OLD BOB'S BIRDS

OLD BOB'S BIRDS

By C.K. Thompson

(author of "King of the Ranges," etc)

20 LIVING BOOK PRESS 17

This edition published 2017
By Living Book Press
147 Durren Rd, Jilliby, 2259
Copyright © The Estate of C.K. Thompson, 1950

The publisher would like to give a huge 'Thank You' to the author's family
for their assistance in making this book available once more.

National Library of Australia Cataloguing-in-Publication entry:

Creator:	Thompson, C.K. (Charles Kenneth), 1904-1980 author
Title:	Old Bob's birds / C.K. Thompson
ISBN:	9780648035640 (paperback)
Target Audience:	For primage school age.
Subjects:	Birds--Australia--Juvenile Fiction.
	Children's stories, Australian.
	Nature stories, Australian.

DEDICATION

To my revered friend, Mrs. BERTHA LAWSON, in appreciation of the assistance she gave me by relating personal experiences with her feathered friends.

Like her husband, the immortal Henry Lawson was, this gracious lady is a passionate lover of the bush and its creatures and she has honored me by developing a special affection for Old Bob's Birds.

FOREWORD

For a great deal of the material in this book I am indebted to my friend and fellow-author, Will Lawson, who, among his many qualities, numbers that of nature-lover and bird-watcher.

Mr. Lawson, while living in an old bush hut of thick bark in the Bargo River Valley, N.S.W., spent a lot of time and trouble observing birds in their native haunts and most of the incidents and happenings in this book arise from his personal observations.

The story of the rock warblers' nest being built inside "Old Bob's" shack, is authentic. Two birds built their nest in Mr. Lawson's hut while the door was shut during his absence, and when he arrived to take up residence, he feared that they would abandon it. Happily, however, they sat on their eggs until three young ones were hatched. His first knowledge of the presence of the nestlings, he told me, was when he felt something light fall on to his shoulder while he was at breakfast one morning. On the floor he saw what he took to be a woolly worm. It was a nestling which he picked up and restored to the nest.

The episode of the two young bird-trappers and that in which "Old Bob" teaches a young magpie how to fly, are taken from my own experiences.

In forwarding me his notes, Mr. Lawson, with what I must call misplaced modesty, wrote that as his literary work lay in other fields, he doubted his ability to weave them into stories for young people. Readers of Mr. Lawson's fine historical romances, sea stories and verse, will not doubt his ability to write upon any subject.

He has, however, laid the charge upon me, and here are "Old Bob's Birds" much as Mr. Lawson told me about them.

C. K. Thompson

Contents

I.	OLD BOB'S CHILDREN	1
II.	THE ROCK WARBLERS' NEST	10
III.	WILLIE WAGTAIL	21
IV.	PEOPLE OF THE SWAMPS	30
V.	THE TRAPPERS	38
VI.	THE BLUE WREN'S GUEST	47
VII.	SLOW WINGS, THE PEEWIT	53
VIII.	OLD JIM CROW	59
IX.	THE DIVE BOMBERS	66
X.	THE HILLS OF HAPPINESS	74
XI.	LENNIE THE LYRE-BIRD	86
XII.	HOOK-BEAK, THE BUTCHER	92
XIII.	BLUE-EYES, THE BOWER BIRD	98
XIV.	BOOMER THE BITTERN	102

Chapter I
OLD BOB'S CHILDREN

DOWN along the bank of the reed-fringed creek that wound its way through the bushlands to empty itself into the wide swamp, old Bob the swagman had built a hut. Half-hidden by dense scrub, the hut, a structure of strong saplings and thick bark, had, for many years, served the old man as a kind of rest home in his wanderings.

Nobody knew if old Bob had any other name, neither did they trouble to inquire. He was just "Old Bob" to everyone, large and small, and he was a general favorite in the neighborhood.

A typical sundowner was old Bob, and his home was where he happened to be; but he regarded the old bark hut as his holiday camp— the little peaceful haven to which he returned to relax after many weeks, sometimes months, on the track. Shunning the cities and towns, even the larger hamlets, the swagman invariably followed the river. It was his habit to make his way down the right bank, doing odd jobs at various stations and farms for weeks on end, and then to return along the left bank, until eventually he reached the old bark hut. There, with a sigh of contentment, he would drop his swag in a corner and live quietly until the urge came upon him once more to seek the open road and camp beneath the stars in distant places.

Not far away from the bark hut stood the farm-house where the swagman's young friend Roddy lived. The cultivated paddocks about it stood out sharply against the brown and green of the grasslands and the bush. Roddy was a lively youngster, a true bush boy, and what had first attracted old Bob to him was the lad's passionate love for the birds of the bush. Bob himself was a born naturalist, and one of his greatest joys was to study the lives and habits of the beautiful little creatures with which Nature had so bountifully endowed the creek and scrublands where the bark hut stood.

The old man loved the birds—all of them; but his love was not an unreasoning passion. They were his children, he often told Roddy, and he knew that, like children, the feathered songsters had their little faults, their individual weaknesses as well as virtues, and he was, in his queer old way, very glad of it.

"There is nothing perfect in this world, my boy," he told young Roddy. "If all things were perfect it would be a dull and very uninteresting place to live in. And it would not be natural."

Every bird that dwelt near the hut, and every visiting songster from other regions, enjoyed old Bob's special protection; and when he was away following the rivers, the guardianship was handed over to Roddy, and his sister Susan.

And it was a most important guardianship, too. There were so many birds to watch over. Old Bob insisted that he had no favorites but treated them all alike. Roddy, on the other hand, was inclined to place the kookaburra on a pinnacle.

"I can't understand why you like old Jack more than the others," old Bob said one day while they were seated on a log outside the hut discussing their feathered friends.

"I think it is because he is so happy and lively," replied the boy. "Nothing ever seems to worry him. He is always laughing."

"Yes; and not always because he is happy," said the swaggie with some scorn. "He often laughs at other folks' misfortunes. One day I was carrying some sticks into the hut and I tripped and fell over a stump. That wasn't very funny, but Jack and his mate laughed so much, you'd think they were at a circus and I was the clown."

"He might have been laughing at something else," suggested the boy.

"Mebbe," said old Bob briefly. "Yes. He might have been laughing at the way some people, human people I mean, praise him to the skies for being such a fine snake killer. He might kill little ones, but in all the years I've been on the track I've never seen a kookaburra pick up a big snake, fly into the air with it and drop it, and keep on doing it until the thing was dead. What is more, I've never met anyone who has seen him do it."

"That doesn't mean that kookaburras don't kill snakes like that," said Roddy.

"No, I know that," admitted the sundowner. "I'm just giving you my own personal experiences."

"However," he went on after a short pause, "old Jack Kookaburra is a good example of what I told you about no person or bird being perfect. Lots of human people, mostly them that have never been in the bush, look on old Jack as a hero without any faults at all. I like old Jack because he has a lot of little faults, and I tell you, my boy, that bird is always laughing because of the silly things people believe about him. The fact is, he is no gentleman."

"Exactly what do you mean, Bob?" asked Roddy. "I know that kookaburras sometimes steal nestlings from the nests of other birds and I know that they often take chickens from farms; but they also eat mice, rats and sparrows, which are pests around a place."

"You're right there, Roddy. They eat snakes, lizards, frogs, yabbies and all sorts of things," said Bob. "What I meant by saying Jack isn't a gentleman is this: he is a thief. Do you know what I once saw a kookaburra do? A blue crane had caught a fish over in the swamps and before he could swallow it, Jack or one of his mates swooped out of a tree and collared it out of the crane's beak."

"But kookaburras go fishing themselves," protested Roddy. "They are really kingfishers, you know."

"Ever seen a kookaburra catch a fish?" demanded the old man.

"No," confessed the boy.

"I did once, and once only," retorted the swagman. "It was at a waterhole that was nearly dried up. There were some little fish in the mudhole, just tiddlers about two inches long, and this kookaburra collected three of them while I was watching. Don't try to tell me old Jack is a fisherman!"

As if in complete endorsement of the old man's words, a sudden burst of hearty laughter rang out from the high branches of the tree under which they were sitting. Glancing up, man and boy observed two kookaburras

—sober-looking, Quaker-like birds whose plumage did not match at all their happy natures.

"What did I tell you?" asked old Bob meaningly, and the boy smiled.

There were many kinds of birds in old Bob's "family." They were all very busy, either searching for food or building nests or feeding their youngsters. Apart from Jack Kookaburra, Bluey the parrot and Maggie the magpie—loud notes in the feathered choir with others of their kith and kin sometimes joining in—there were the softer voices. One of the smallest—very small indeed, was Witloo the diamond sparrow. With his tiny comrades, Witloo played among the leaves and branches, feeding on insects and generally conducting himself in innocent fashion. Sometimes he sang "wit-e-chu" in faint, sweet tones, at other times his song was "wit-loo" with a long pause between the two notes, which were clear, yet so tuned that when he was near, it sounded as if he were far away. He stood on his small toes to whistle "wit," and then turned his head for "loo."

Then there was Blue Jacket, the kingfisher, a cousin of Jack Kookaburra. He dwelt mostly on branches overhanging the creek, into which he would dive after fish, patrolling the banks and eagerly seeking places where the fishing was good. When he flew along just skimming the water, he was a lovely gleam of color. His cinnamon-tinted breast was reflected in the clear water, while his rich, royal blue back and wings were like a flash of flame.

Another bright dweller in old Bob's sanctuary was Ring Coachman, the whistler, who came to hunt insects on the trunks of trees. His clear, bold whistle sometimes ended with a ringing sound like the crack of a whip. His rival, who rarely showed himself, was Ping, the stockwhip bird, who lived away from the farmlands. Sometimes he ventured close in the early mornings and his distinctive note had a real whip-crack at the end.

Perhaps most striking of all was Gorgeous, the flying Coachman. His loud "clink-clank" echoed down the leafy avenues and the flash of his gold and black plumage made rich color among the trees. He was a bird that seemed always to be in a hurry, and he had need to be. Honey and pollen were his favorite foods and as there were many of his species and not much of either delicacy in any one tree, Gorgeous had to cover a great deal of bushland each day. He did so, his noisy voice waking the echoes and the flashing gold of his feathers challenging the sunshine.

Blue Bonnet the wren was a quiet little fellow compared with such noisy folk, but his song was sweet, making real music; and the royal blue of his plumage was like a rich gem in the sombre setting of the scrub. Slow Wings, the peewit, whose song was harsh and flat by day, yet sweet as a bell at dawn, and Friar the leatherhead, added their voices to the feathered choir. They were hardly in the top flight of songsters except that Slow Wings, before dawn was fairly born, would warble "bob-o-link" with wonderfully liquid notes.

One of the worst of old Bob's "children" was Hook-beak, the butcher-bird. All the little finches, wrens and other small fry would have been happy creatures could old Bob have banned this terror, but, as the old man once said, Hook-beak had his place in nature and nature knew best.

Hook-beak was a killer who preyed on the smaller birds, stealing their nestlings and even making a meal out of any unfortunate parent who came within range of his terrible bill. The little songsters could not fight him as did Jack Kookaburra.

But Hook-beak partially compensated for his murderous habits by the wonderful quality of his song. It was one of the sweetest in the bush, rivalling even that of his cousin, the magpie, whose carollings at dawn and dusk, and sometimes on moonlight nights were of magnificent choral splendor. Neither, in old Bob's opinion, did Hook-beak outshine Browneyes the thrush in vocal prowess. His song was a delight to the ear, gentle, and very much like himself. The thrush was no predatory slayer, certainly not like Gar Gar the sparrowhawk, who would swoop from the skies on little birds and young farmyard chickens.

New arrivals, or visitors, to old Bob's sanctuary had no need to provide their own hospitality. They found it in nature's lavish store.

One fine evening there came a flash of green and pale blue among the trees, and a short bird with a long bill alighted on a limb not far from the hut and called very quickly, "Tee-tee-tee!" From another tree a hundred yards away, the call was answered, and the first bird hurried off to join his mate. They were sacred kingfishers, correctly called Halcyon, a name bestowed upon the family in years long past because the birds always arrived in the halcyon days of summer. Soon they would be nesting in old Bob's sanctuary. Then, weeks later, they would lead their young ones away on their endless travelling, for these birds were rovers.

Sometimes from the river pools far away would sound the croaking call of Longneck the crested grebe, who never stayed long in old Bob's domain. He loved a more secluded place in which to nest—amongst long reeds by far-away pools. But the deep voice of Boomer the bittern was often heard after darkness had fallen. It was hard to determine just where Boomer was, for his call seemed to echo far over the swamplands. Brown Wings the harrier would linger in the dusk to try to catch water fowl unawares. There were many living in the swamps, including Bald Coot, a water hen with long red legs, who nested on a small island.

And, as the moon rose, silvering the bush, the swamps and the creek with her soft, white light, far away in the distant hills would sound the quavering call "wee-lo" of the stone curlew. Mournfully would come the ghostly wail of the swamp curlew, which, with his kith and kin, ran about in the moonlight by the marshy shore.

Like a phantom in the still night air, Boo-book the owl flew on silent wings, while Willie Wagtail, safe in the thick sheoaks, taunted him as he passed. Other birds, even Blue-beak the tree martin, who pride himself on being a fighter, were not as bold as Willie Wagtail at night, especially when the sharp, quick hunting cry of White-throat the nightjar told of the presence of another slayer. Woe betide any small birds who, terrified by the cries of the prowlers, sought safer quarters. Yet it was hard to sit still on a tree branch, no matter how secluded that branch was, when the "hoo-hooha-ha" of the screech-owl came like a woman's scream, mingled with sobbing. It was, however, the owl's business to scare small birds from their hiding places, and if the small birds refused to be scared, the owls went hungry.

Night could be terrible in the bush.

High on a branch, Jack Kookaburra, Maggie Magpie and such aristocrats, heard the calls of the hunters and treated them with contempt. No prowlers would dare to attack them.

As for Jack Kockaburra, who was a bit of a killer himself, his sovereignty ended with the going down of the sun. In daylight he would fight goannas, snakes, butcher-birds and fellow killers. At night he could do nothing—except sleep. Which he did.

Chapter II
THE ROCK WARBLERS' NEST

OLD BOB had been away for several weeks on one of his periodical walkabouts, but Roddy, expecting him back any day, had got into the habit of strolling over to the hut to see if his old friend was again in residence.

Thus it was that, noticing the door of the hut open one morning, the boy gave a joyful shout and ran over. Sure enough, the old man was there, eating his breakfast and in a happy mood. He waved a fork in welcome to his young friend, who immediately sat down on an old box and began to ply Bob with questions about his adventures on the track.

"Nothing of interest this trip, young feller," replied Bob, "Nothing to report or make a song about."

"Gee, Bob, talking about songs," said Roddy eagerly, "I've got a song about you!"

"About me?" exclaimed the swagman, laying down his knife and fork in surprise.

"Well, er, it's not exactly a song, Bob. It's a piece of poetry I made up about you," said the boy. "Leastwise, Susan helped me a bit. So did Dad."

Old Bob looked at him sternly.

"Been writing poetry about me, huh?" he asked. "I don't hold with poetry. I think them poet fellers are all mad."

Roddy blushed and looked confused. Old Bob immediately saw that he had hurt the boy's feelings and was quick to make amends.

"Only pulling your leg, Roddy," he mumbled. "Matter of fact I like poetry."

"Do you really, Bob?" asked the boy eagerly. "Would you like me to read this one of mine to you?"

"I'm all ears," Bob assured him.

"No, you're not, Bob," laughed Roddy. "Your ears are a nice size."

"Don't get funny, young feller-me-lad," said the swagman sternly. "Read your poetry."

Roddy fumbled in his pockets, produced a rather grubby piece of paper which he had been carrying around with him for some time, smoothed it out on the table, and then glanced up at the old man.

"It's called, 'Old Bob,' " he announced.

"Go ahead," said the swagman and Roddy did so-

> *What is it sets the wild birds singing—*
> *The magpies' call and the peewits' notes,*
> *The joyous song of the wild thrush ringing—*
> *A chorus sweet from a hundred throats?*
> *A whisper has gone through bushland, thrilling*
> *Each songster's heart in sun or rain;*
> *To greet their friend they all come trilling:*
> *"Old Bob's back in his hut again!"*

The swagman's back from the rivers sweeping,
From breezy ridges and shining plain,
Where the men and teams are busy reaping
The heavy heads of the golden grain.
Far and away has Old Bob been roaming,
A wanderer ever in life is he;
Yet he'll be happy today in coming
Back to the realm of swamp and tree.

The swallows know him and pass the word on,
The parrots cry, "Bob's here once more."
Surely in this is a bushman's guerdon,
Meeting his birdland friends of yore!
He will sleep tonight with happy dreaming,
While his fire burns red and the smoke will be
Blue in the golden morning gleaming,
For every bird in the bush to see.

There was silence in the hut for a few moments after the boy had finished reading. Then:

"Roddy, my lad, that was really fine. That was really beautiful," said the old swagman in a sincere voice.

"I'm glad you liked it," replied Roddy in tones of happiness.

"I did and I want a copy of it, too," said Old Bob nodding his head vigorously. "Boy," he went on, "that's the second great thrill I've had since I've been back this time. The first happened when I landed here only last night."

"Is that so? What happened?" asked Roddy. "Did some robber get in while you were away and steal your things?"

Old Bob laughed loudly.

"Robbers wouldn't find much here to steal, Roddy," he grinned. "No, I ain't been robbed. It was something in the hut itself that gave me the thrill, lad. Can you see anything different about the old place?"

Roddy stared about him, examining every part of the hut, and then had to confess that he could see no alterations or additions.

"Of course you can't!" said the old man with a chuckle. "You looked everywhere except in the right place. You're sitting right under it. Look upwards, son!"

Roddy did so. At first he saw nothing and then his keen eyes alighted upon a roundish ball of bark fibre, grass, cobwebs and the old egg-sacs of spiders.

"A nest!" he exclaimed in delighted surprise. "What kind is it, Bob?"

"Rock warblers'," the old man answered. "They must have built it just after I went away. Found a safe place in here, I reckon, away from butcher-birds, hawks and other feathered robbers. Have a look inside, Roddy, and you will see Mrs. Rock Warbler at home."

The excited boy stood up on the old box and peered into the hooded side-entrance of the nest. There he could just make out the tiny rufous-brown head of the little bird, which stared back at him with fearless bright eyes.

"Isn't it wonderful how they have built it?" he said. "See how they have woven the bits of bark and string and cobwebs and how neatly it is fixed to the bark roof of the hut. Did you see them doing it, Bob?"

"No," replied the swagman. "It was built while I was away, as I told you. But I've seen plenty of these nests in other places and have watched the little birds at work. They certainly know their jobs."

"What are rock warblers?" asked Roddy, resuming his seat on the box. "I've never seen them before, that I can remember."

"They are a sort of wren, or robin," replied Bob. "I don't know much about the book part of it, or how those scientist fellers would describe them. All I know is that they are friendly little souls, like blue wrens and old Jacky Whiter. Rock birds often nest in trees and old huts like this one, but most of them fancy caves.

"Yes," he added, after a short pause, "I've seen many of 'em in that wild country up around the Hawkesbury River. They like to build their nests in the sandstone caves."

He broke off as a small bird flew in at the door clung to the side entrance of the nest and passed an insect from his beak to his mate.

"See that?" exclaimed Bob in delight. "Notice how he feeds her? I reckon those two birds will always nest in here now."

"They're not a bit afraid of us, are they?" said Roddy.

"Not a scrap," replied Bob. "No birds in the bush are afraid of me because they always know somehow that I'll never hurt them. They ain't afraid of you either, my lad. Just look at that, now!"

The little male bird, after fluttering around the hut, had perched fearlessly upon Roddy's shoulder. The lad stood perfectly still, his young soul thrilling. He felt the slight breeze from the little wings as the rock warbler suddenly left him and darted through the doorway.

"Lovely little creatures," said the old swagman. "And to think that there are people living in this here country who have no love for the birds. I can't understand some of 'em, Roddy, really I can't."

"Neither can I," the boy replied.

"Of course, it is mostly the young boys who never think what they are doing who cause the greatest damage among the birds," went on the old man. "Thoughtless young fellers with their catapults and their bird traps and so on. Thank goodness, when they grow up they alter, or else there wouldn't be any birds left in the bush."

"The birds sometimes kill each other, Bob," pointed out Roddy.

"So they do, so they do," nodded Bob.

Suddenly the old man paused, his eyes fixed on the doorway. A big, handsome bird, silver-grey, with a black cap and throat, had winged to the door. It saw Bob and Roddy, swerved and clung to the bark of the old chimney. From this precarious perch, its sharp, fierce eyes glared at the nest for a moment, and then the bird vanished among the trees outside.

"Did you see that?" breathed Roddy.

"Yes, a dashed butcherbird," said old Bob briefly.

"What do you think he would have done?"

"Done? What do they do?" growled the swaggie. "Do all the other birds if they get the chance. One of the worst robbers in the bush, that butcher-bird. Real bushrangers, they all are. Lucky we were here or he'd have got that little rock warbler."

He looked at Roddy sternly.

"Now let this be a lesson to you, my lad," he said. "If

you are ever in this hut, never leave the door open when you go out. Them birds built here when the place was shut up. They believed they were safe. It is up to us to see that they are safe."

"I like that," said Roddy indignantly. "It is not me who leaves the door open. Just mind that you don't." He said that, because old Bob was inclined to be forgetful and absent-minded at times, just like most old sundowners who spent all their lives in the bush and on the track, carrying their swags and camping wherever they happened to be when night fell.

"Me?" exclaimed old Bob, with equal indignation, "Don't you worry about me, youngster. It's you young blokes who forget things, not old men like me. No, sir!"

He then announced his determination to remain in the hut until the warblers had reared their family. He would not go away again on the track until this had been done.

During the days that passed, the old man spent a lot of his time watching the birds and their nest and he appeared to get quite a lot of fun out of it. Sometimes Roddy, visiting the hut, found the old chap lying on his bunk reading, or sitting at his table, while the little birds flew in and out as if he were not there—or as if he were a very old and intimate friend.

One day the boy arrived at the hut to find the old man holding a wee object in his work-hardened hand. When he saw Roddy he said:

"Just you look at that. Found it on the floor. Something hit me on the shoulder. I looked up and then at the ground, and there it was."

"What is it, Bob?" demanded the boy.

"Young 'un, just hatched. Them careless birds must have shoved it out somehow."

"You don't think they did it on purpose, do you, Bob?" asked Roddy anxiously. He hated to think that a bird could be so callous.

"Shouldn't think so. Probably rolled it out as one of them was leaving. Anyway, we'll soon see, because I'm going to put it back again with its mate. Only two of them hatched out of the eggs. If the birds throw it out again I'll know it was deliberate and I'll have something to say to 'em."

"What?" asked the boy with a smile.

"You'll see."

At the moment both birds were absent from the nest. With their eggs hatched, they could afford to have a spell from setting. Gently the old swaggie replaced the fallen nestling. The small body was still warm. He and Roddy then sat down again to watch what would happen.

It was not long before one of the parent birds returned and entered the nest. Nothing happened.

"Do you think the poor little thing will die?" asked Roddy.

"Don't know. I'm not a bird doctor, but I reckon not. Careless things, some birds are. Almost as bad as some human beings. Fancy them dropping a young one out of the nest like that."

"Perhaps they meant to. Maybe it was sick," said the boy.

"Well, that bird that went into the nest just now didn't throw the nipper out again, so I guess it was an accident," said Bob.

A few days later when Roddy called again at the hut, old Bob beckoned him over to the nest.

"Guess I can answer your question for sure now," he said. "Stand on the box and have a peep into the nest," he invited.

Roddy did so and when his eyes became accustomed to the gloom, he saw two very healthy-looking little fledglings sitting there with beaks wide open hissing softly for food. They were not the least bit afraid of their human watchers.

As Roddy stepped down from the box, one of the parent birds flew into the hut and, clinging to the nest with its claws, deftly fed an insect to one of the voracious youngsters. Hardly had it vanished outside the hut again than the second parent arrived.

"They're doing that all day," commented old Bob. "Regular hungry pair of young 'uns they've hatched."

He broke off and grinned.

"Won't there be some fun when mum and dad toss the kids out of home," he said with a chuckle.

Roddy looked startled.

"But I thought you said it was an accident last time?" he asked.

"So it was, but it won't be an accident when the young 'uns have all their feathers. They'll be tossed out all right."

"But why?"

"To teach them to fly, of course, me lad," old Bob told him. "In about a week, they'll do it, you'll see. Come back here next week and watch the fun."

"Will you be here?" asked Roddy.

"Will I be here? Of course I'll be here. Do you think I want the rats or owls or butcher birds to get them there young 'uns when they fly out?" said the swaggie indignantly. "Maybe they wouldn't be able to get back to the nest; then they'd make a first class meal for some thieving rat or bird."

After that, Roddy made it a point to call into the hut each day. At last the great moment arrived—the morning he was greeted by old Bob with, "It's happened, young feller." The old chap was very excited and so were the birds who were dashing hither and thither and chirping to their young ones.

"They've tossed them out, Roddy!" shouted old Bob. "The youngsters are around here somewhere. See if you can locate 'em."

Roddy had trouble in finding the young birds. Eventually he ran one to earth outside in a lean-to. The other had managed to get into the low branches of a tree. He tried to catch them both, but they eluded his out-stretched hands, to flutter uncertainly back into the hut. One aimed for the nest, missed the direction and was heading straight for the fire when the old swaggie shot out a hand and grabbed the bird in mid-air.

"Holy snakes!" he yelled. "That was close!"

He carried the little bird carefully to the nest and replaced it. Roddy chased the other and bailed it up in a corner. Picking it up he, too, put it in the nest. The parent birds seemed to be pleased to have their young ones back safely and fluttered around Bob and Roddy as if they were twin Saint Francises, the patron saints of birds.

"Look what would have happened if I hadn't been here," said the swaggie. "That little beggar would have been burned as sure as eggs is eggs."

"But," Roddy pointed out, "if you hadn't been here there wouldn't have been a fire."

"Maybe not, but there would have been hawks and butcher-birds."

"Hawks and other robbers couldn't have got in with the door shut," said Roddy, teasing the old man.

"Dash me buttons, lad, you looking for an argument?" snorted old Bob. "Hang it all, I'm glad I was here anyway, if only to stop you getting up to some funny business with them little birds."

In a few days the young birds could fly quite well and as soon as he was satisfied that they could look after themselves, old Bob announced his intention of going off "on the wallaby"—a trip away on the track.

"Always keep the door of the hut shut," he warned Roddy before he left. "Those rock warblers will nest there again, you mark my words!"

He was right for, when Roddy visited the hut one day long afterwards, there were three fresh eggs in the nest.

Chapter III
WILLIE WAGTAIL

IT was a warm, moonlit night and, the milking done and the evening meal over, Roddy considered that it would be a shame to spend the hours before bedtime reading or loafing around the farmhouse. It was just the night for a short stroll and he decided to walk over to old Bob's hut to see how the old man was faring. It was almost a week since he had been at the hut, and found old Bob still away.

His mother raised no objection so, whistling to Tiger to come along if he wanted to, the boy hurried along the old bush path, Tiger racing ahead and investigating hollow logs and clumps of bushes. Tiger had the fixed impression that he was a hunting dog and that the creatures of the bush were in existence wholly for his benefit and as a tribute to his sporting tastes. In the whole of his rather short life he had never accomplished anything more outstanding than chasing a rabbit up a hollow log and a goanna up a gum tree; but he was a true optimist and forever hoped that one day a grand adventure would befall him.

The swagman greeted Roddy warmly.

"Well, sonny-me-lad, you're almost a stranger," he said. "Come on in, you and Tiger, too. You're just in time for a good feed of damper and roast duck. And maybe there'll be a bone or two for Tiger."

"Where did you get the duck, Bob?" asked Roddy curiously.

"I never stole it, anyway," retorted the swaggie. "It came from the swamp. I was down there this afternoon and it was silly enough to get in the way of my rifle. Come on, my lad. Sit down and wire in!'

Tiger, who didn't care a scrap where the duck came from as long as he got some tasty portions of it, barked and wagged his tail. Old Bob rewarded him, not with a bare bone, but with a generous helping of delicious meat. Tiger, who had no manners, swallowed it whole and demanded more. He got it.

Though Roddy had had his tea, boy-like he was still hungry and he needed no second invitation to "wire into" the duck and damper. For some time the only sound heard in the hut apart from the crackling of the fire, was the champing of three sets of jaws as man, boy and dog did justice to the meal.

After the things had been cleared away, Bob and Roddy sat down to talk. Tiger retired to the old hearthstone and even though the night was warm, stretched out and promptly went to sleep—to dream of bigger and better bones and of that great hunting adventure he hoped to have some time.

"Summer's going," old Bob commented as he lighted his battered old pipe by thrusting a stick into the fire and conveying the blazing end to the bowl.

"Saw some black swans on the swamps today and the swallows are massing ready to depart. I've seen 'em."

"So have I," nodded Roddy. "It won't be long before all the visiting birds go."

"All I wish is that one little devil would depart and forget to come back again," exclaimed the old swagman. "It's bad luck that he never shifts much. Kept me awake most of last night, singing out and chattering away, just like a shearers' delegate."

"What's a shearer's delegate, Bob? Some sort of a bird?" asked the boy, and the old man chuckled heartily

"No, Roddy. He's a bloke who represents the shearers at meetings and they never select a cove unless he can talk the leg off an iron pot."

"But what bird was it that kept you awake? What did he say?" Roddy asked.

"He kept screeching out 'It's a political question'. I roared back that I was tired and wanted to go to sleep, and he screeched 'did-yah-did-yah-did-yah,' " grunted Bob.

"Oh, you mean Willie Wagtail!" laughed Roddy. "But what he says is 'sweet pretty creature.' "

"He might to you, but never to me," declared Bob. "I don't know what I've done to that bird, but he's always trying to get me into an argument. All night he kept it up and I threw a drayload of stones at him, I did."

"Did it make him keep quiet?"

"No, it didn't," exclaimed old Bob in disgust.

"But he wasn't just calling out to annoy you, Bob," said the boy. "He was just warning the owls and other night birds that he was awake and ready to protect his nest if they felt like attacking him. I don't suppose he even knew you were here."

"No, I don't suppose he did. He thought it was the owls who threw all those stones at him," said the swagman sarcastically.

"I suppose he prefers dodging the stones to dodging the owls," grinned the boy.

"Listen here, young feller, I don't care why he sings out. All I know is that if he doesn't shut up, I'll move on somewhere else. A man has got to have some sleep, you know!"

"Why don't you shoot him?" asked Roddy, knowing quite well what the answer would be.

"Shoot him? Me, shoot a harmless little bird that is only protecting his nest?" roared Bob. "What do you think I am?"

Roddy grinned, but did not answer, and presently he announced that it was time he was going home.

"Well, good night, son," said the old man. "When you pass Willie Wagtail's tree on the way, you tell him what I said, won't you?"

"I will," promised Roddy and, whistling to Tiger, said a cheery good-night and left the hut. Tiger, who had been dreaming that he had killed a pack of wild dingoes on his own, was pulled back into the humdrum old world; and, with a little whine of disappointment, he followed his young master.

Roddy did not know where Willie Wagtail's nest was, but as he walked along the old bush track, the little black and white bird hurled a shrill insult at him. He stopped and examined the tree nearest to him. In the leaf-filtered moonlight, he could just make out a small nest wedged in the fork of a sheoak.

Willie was nearby and on sentry duty.

"Sweet pretty creature," said Roddy, but Willie ignored his blandishments.

"You'd better keep quiet tonight, Willie," said the lad "Old Bob wouldn't hurt you deliberately, but if he does throw stones at you, one of them might find a mark. What are you going to do?"

The little black and white bird swayed on the twig in silence for a moment and then:

"That's a political question," he screeched.

"It's a question I'll answer with a brick if you don't shut up," came a roar from the hut. Roddy laughed and went on his way, leaving his old friend Bob and his feathered friend Willie to settle the argument between themselves.

As he walked steadily along, his ears were assailed by the deep-throated croaks of bull-frogs from the creek that ran near the hut and the wagtail's nest. The thought crossed his mind that old Bob would have to put plugs in his ears if he wanted absolute quiet in which to sleep.

Picking up a few stones, the boy tossed them into the creek, causing a sudden hush of the froggy chorus.

Willie was silent for the time being, so if the swagman could drop off quickly, all would be well. But it was not to be; for, hardly had the boy walked a few yards than the frogs started up again in full voice and Willie commenced a new political debate with himself—and the owls.

It was very late at night ere the frog-chorus died away. Old Bob, his blankets wrapped round his head to keep out the nocturnal noises, slept peacefully.

Even Willie Wagtail, tired after so much vocal argument, was half-asleep near his nest. The whole bushland seemed to be at rest.

But appearances are deceptive. The preying creatures

of the night do not advertise their presence and their intentions. On soft ghostly wings the owls and nightjars were abroad, hunting and preying, their small victims dying violently in their sleep; those spotted menaces, the tiger cat and his smaller brother, the native cat, were stalking and obeying the laws of the bush—the weak must go down that the strong may survive.

It was a slight scratching sound on the trunk of the tree in which his nest was placed that brought the sleepy wagtail into complete wakefulness. Peering down through the needle-like leaves he saw yellow eyes shining up at him. They belonged to a brown animal with white spots all over his body except his tail—a native cat.

Like others of its kind, this wildcat was completely fearless and possessed a bold intelligence. In its time it had preyed upon mice, rats, rabbits and large birds and a mere wagtail meant nothing to it. It knew the nest was there and it hoped that there were young ones in it. It knew, too, that Willie was on guard and his mate was on the nest. If there were two young ones in the nest, that would yield a meal of four birds with a bit of luck. Of course, Willie, being awake, might escape, but a quick spring would easily dispose of the mother bird and then the nestlings would be there for the eating.

The native cat had it all planned out. It treated with complete contempt any suggestion that the wagtail might prove a doughty antagonist. A momentary nuisance, possibly, but nothing more.

Willie sat there watching as the cat commenced to climb the tree. Steadily it came on, but the bird made no sign until the animal reached the first branch.

With a terrific screech that made old Bob turn in his blankets, Willie hurled himself at the spotted intruder, aiming for its eyes. He was so quick that the cat felt the brushing of little wings before it knew it was being attacked. Alarmed by her mate's cries, the mother bird left the nest and joined in the fray. As they both dived and pecked and fluttered around the cat's head, that annoyed animal waved a wicked clawed paw in an ineffectual attempt to tear them out of the air. They were far too agile for him, however, so he gave it up to concentrate upon the main business of the night—an investigation of the nest and its contents.

The cat had had to revise his first estimates of his likely bird meal. He knew that it was most unlikely now that he would have either Willie or his mate. He must, therefore, depend upon the nest and if that were empty, then he would go hungry. This thought spurred the cat on. He decided to waste no time in fending off the parent birds. After all, they could do him but little damage, he considered. So, in a deadly-purposeful way, he resumed his climb.

Again and again the two wagtails attacked like dive-bombers and in spite of his determination to allow nothing to distract him, the cat was forced now and again to freeze to the tree and hang on with three paws while he fended off the attacks with the fourth.

Willie's blood was up under the excitement of the affair, but his mate was distracted. Her small bird mind was divided. It was urging her to stay at the nest and protect the young ones from this cat and any hunting night birds, and also urging her to take direct action against the spotted menace climbing upwards.

Her mind was made up for her when she heard the hooting of an owl nearby. She flew to the nest and crouched on it in fear and trembling, allowing Willie to bear alone the brunt of the battle with the native cat.

At length the animal reached the branch on which the nest was situated. The spotted terror crouched on the limb and snarled at Willie who had come to rest near the nest. It was about six feet from where the cat crouched ready to rush along the limb and the Wagtail knew that it was now or never. If he could not get rid of the menace, then his home and possibly his mate, would be gone for good.

With a chirp of desperation, Willie sprang into the air and with a continuous screech hurled himself at the cat. That animal saw him coming and raised a wicked paw. Willie struck him right between the eyes, but the blow was nothing to the tough animal.

Round and round flew the little bird, its loud cries echoing through the silent bush. Old Bob, who had been awakened by the row, lay still in his bunk, until he could stand it no longer.

Leaping from the bed, he rushed to the door, threw it open and hurled a string of abuse at the bird. Then, stooping down, he picked up a huge stone and flung it madly in the direction of the bird uproar. The stone soared high, crashed through twigs and leaves and, catching the native cat fair in the ribs, dislodged it from the branch. Scrambling, snarling and clawing at the branches and the trunk, the animal lost its balance completely and fell to the ground. It was up immediately and away through the scrub.

"Shut up, you noisy wagtail, or I'll come over and

wring your neck for you!" howled old Bob, who knew nothing of the native cat.

"Sweet pretty creature, sweet pretty creature!" screeched Willie in high delight.

"Shut up, I tell you!" the swaggie bellowed. "It ain't a political question at all. The question is, do I get any sleep to-night? Shut up!"

And when a stone sang past the nest, Willie did shut up. He went and sat near his mate, who, woman-like now that the danger was past, scolded him for being half-asleep when on sentry duty Willie, in his bird way, let her know that he had not been asleep. This she rejected and told him that he was a poor sort of nest guardian to allow a native cat to come so close before he detected its presence.

Willie screeched back, not unreasonably, that even if he had detected the cat two miles away, it would not have improved him as a warrior. The cat was big and he was little and only for the old human being in the hut, heaven knows what would have happened.

But Mrs. Wagtail had a grouch and insisted on airing it.

"Oh gosh, the two of them are at it now," groaned old Bob, as the screeches assailed his ears.

"Will you shut up, you two?" he roared. "For two pins, I'd climb that tree and stick a match in your nest!"

Willie and his mate lapsed into silence and with a grunt old Bob returned to his bunk and was soon asleep again.

"I ought to pull the feathers out of your tail and then you'd have nothing to wag, vain creature that you are," Mrs. Wagtail suddenly screeched at Willie.

"Sweet pretty creature," sang Willie softly and soothingly.

Chapter IV
PEOPLE OF THE SWAMPS

LYING face downwards amongst the ferns and long grasses, Roddy watched, in fascinated silence, the scene in the pool below him. At this spot the creek, which meandered lazily through the swamplands, met a swelling rise in the land and skirted its base, scouring a deep hole.

In this deep pool a black duck was patiently training her brood of ducklings in the important art of aquatics, and it was this little domestic scene that the boy found so absorbing. He admired the speed with which they darted hither and thither, and smiled at their attempts to stand on their diminutive heads as they tried to feed on water plants growing beneath the surface. They were self-satisfied swimmers, these downy little ducklings, and Roddy could not but smile at the little tails he saw elevated as their owners thrust their head under water in imitation of their mother.

The birds that dwelt in the wide swamplands had always held a subtle fascination for the boy. When he was but a wee child lying snugly at home in his cot he used to hear them calling to each other at night—so eerily and sadly it seemed to his young ears. At times he felt inclined to creep from the silent farmhouse and visit them in their haunts, but had never been able to pluck up the courage.

Indeed, even now that he was a big boy, Roddy had never ventured near the swamps at night; but he often went there during the sunny daylight hours to watch the water birds.

These swamplands covered a very large area. Far, far away they stretched, wide and level and gay with reeds and tall grasses waving in the wind. It was a scene which altered in composition with the changing sunlight and shadows; sometimes brilliant, sometimes drab but, to the boy, always filled with life and so utterly satisfying to a soul as close to nature as he was. When the breeze rippled the brown water and shadows chased each other across the inland seascape, the water-folk seemed to be at their liveliest.

Perhaps it was their exhilaration that nature was so alive around them, striking a responsive chord in their wild natures.

Roddy knew most of the swamp people. Bald Coot was one of his favorites, though he disliked the unattractive name of this handsome swamp hen. Overhead sweeping to and fro on tireless wings, the harrier swamp-hawk kept fierce eyes trained on the earth and water below, ready to swoop down upon any unsuspecting creature and especially unprotected eggs, chickens or ducklings.

Spurwing the plover also haunted the swamplands. Roddy liked him because his loud call when alarmed placed every other bird upon its guard. Thus, marauding human beings with their guns and dogs gained small hunting profit when Spurwing was alert. And his chicks were a delight to the eye; independent little fellows able to run soon after being hatched. Spurwing and his mate, however, kept strict discipline and at the first sign of danger, a call from either parent saw each little chick immobile with head on the ground until all danger had passed.

But in this regard they were in no way superior to any of the swamplands people. Obedience among the youngsters was the general rule. No chick disobeyed its parents, for to do so would mean the end of all things. There were too many dangers to face—from the air, from the earth and from the waters below.

Though Roddy knew the curlew, the black swan, the peewit that patrolled the edges of the swamp and most of the other creatures there, Boomer the bittern was a stranger. From Old Bob he had learned the habits of this bird but he had never seen him. Boomer would stand with his bill uplifted like the broken branch of a small tree and thus was very hard to detect in his natural surroundings. The boy was determined, however, that one day he would see Boomer. He felt that until he had done so, he would not know the swamplands.

A sight that never lost its fascination for the boy was the arrival at the swamps of the swans. In the spring in a wedge-shaped phalanx they came, swooping down upon the water with a clatter of wings sweeping against the rushes and webbed feet churning the surface.

As the lad lay in the bright sunshine watching the black duck and her brood, he became aware of a menacing shadow crowing and re-crossing the pool. No need for him to look upwards to ascertain the cause. He knew that Brownwings the harrier was on hunting business and that business concerned the duck and her brood.

Looking around him, the lad searched for a stick or stone which he intended to drop into the pool to scare the ducks before the harrier had a chance to strike. There was nothing in reach. Rolling on his back, Roddy stared at the sky. There high in the blue he saw the swamp-hawk poised on outstretched pinions. Suddenly the hunting bird dived like an arrow, straight at the pool.

Quick as he was, however, the black duck had seen that menacing shadow growing larger as the hunter dropped. In a flutter of alarm, she gave the warning quack the young ones knew so well. With amazing speed they scattered, each little duckling to himself; and then, as if at a given signal, they all dived deep, to swim under water until they reached the safety of the dense rushes.

The black duck herself did not rush for cover. She knew she had nothing much to fear from the hawk. That baffled bird, his talons outstretched, clawed nothing but water, and then insult was added to injury when the black duck threw more water into his eyes with her wildly beating wings.

Discomfited, the harrier whirled sullenly aloft again, to take up his station and wait until some more favorable target presented itself. Roddy by this time had found a stone and this he threw at the fluttering menace above. The stone whizzed past its tail and it left that vicinity, presently to hover again over a distant part of the swamps. Then, one by one, the small ducklings reappeared and hurried back to their mother's side, where the family swam about in a manner that reminded Roddy of a fleet of small tugs fussing around an ocean liner.

Now that all seemed safe with the duck family, Roddy

left his vantage place overlooking the pool and made his way by a roundabout path to where he could watch Bald Coot stalking in shallow water on his long red legs, or swimming with smooth gait in deeper places. The swamphen's legs ended in widespread, long-clawed toes which enabled him to walk on mud. He and his mate had established their home on a small islet of rushes and they usually lurked there during the long daylight hours, coming out to feed in the early mornings and late evenings.

Roddy was interested to observe that the bald coots fed like the cockatoos, lifting food from the mud and water to their beaks with one claw while they stood firmly on the other.

They were handsome birds, these swamp-hens with their indigo breasts and shiny black backs. The chicks were odd-looking little things with black bodies, red legs and yellow beaks, but they cared nothing for their appearance as they solemnly imitated their parents in feeding.

Now, although the harrier had been disappointed in his attack on the black duck's brood, that had not meant that he had given up hunting for the day. At that precise moment he was in the air over the swamp-hen's family and he was just awaiting an opportunity to strike.

And that opportunity came when a coot chick, straying away from his parents in search of a tasty morsel, presented what the harrier considered was the perfect target. It was the hawk's own fault that he did not secure that chick. Instead of swooping straight down and seizing the little bird, he stopped half-way, fluttered, and then dropped again—too late.

He had no sooner reached the level of the shallow water than he in his turn was attacked—by a squad of bald coots that charged him like so many long-legged dragoons. The hawk actually got the chick in his talons and was about to rise on his wide wings when the mother coot was on him, striking him with her beak and beating her wings in his face. Her furious onslaught forced him to release his grip on the youngster, which tumbled, unhurt into the water. The harrier, baffled for the second time that day, whirled off into the sky, while the triumphant coots scattered again to feed, their shrill cries ringing like barbed insults in the disgruntled ears of the rising hawk. That bird determined to give up trying to secure a meal of young waterfowl and endeavour to find an unguarded nest filled with eggs.

The sun was setting behind the distant ranges—a warning to Roddy that it was time to go home. Reluctantly he rose from his seat on a grassy bank and was walking away towards the higher ground when he stopped in sudden surprise. Crouched on the ground at his feet was Spurwing the plover. He stood perfectly still and allowed his eyes to wander around the grassland. Presently he saw another plover, then a third. Only the eyes of a bush-trained lad could have detected them. Carefully the boy avoided the birds and walked with eyes averted. He knew that once his eyes met those of one of the plovers the whole flock would take flight. Once the human eye meets that of a wild thing, that wild thing knows that further precaution is wasted and that it has been discovered.

Reaching the higher ground as dusk fell, Roddy turned around for one last look at the swamplands. A solitary plover's call, lonely and sad, floated to his ears, and then the deep note of a bittern throbbed in the still evening air. A pang of regret that he had never seen this bird gave way to a thrill of pleasure when he observed, sharply-etched against the sky, a black wedge which dropped slowly as it approached.

Like weary voyagers, the flock of black swans, honking as they came, circled the swamps and then swept down to the surface of the dark water, vanishing from the lad's sight. He knew, however, that soon they would be busily foraging for a meal after their foodless flight from coastal places.

And as he turned for home, the last thing he heard was the tired laugh of Jack Kookaburra bidding farewell to another day from his termite-nest home in a high stringybark.

That night Roddy heard the voices of the swamp people in his dreams. He saw White Feather, the handsome leader of the black swans, magnificent in his pride as he led his flock on and on through reedy pools; while on the muddy shores, Boomer the bittern led the wading birds in stately procession. Suddenly the black duck seemed to dash right in front of White Feather and his flock, bidding him to leave the swamp and return no more. To the boy's horror, White Feather opened a cavernous mouth and swallowed Black Duck and as she disappeared, she quacked loud and long, waking the boy up.

The lad smiled to himself and turned on his side once again to woo the goddess of sleep, serenaded by the hunting cry of the screech owl trying to startle small birds into flight. The owl was answered by a derisive wagtail intent upon letting the hunter know that he, at least, was on his guard and would not be panicked into unreasoningly flight.

Roddy sighed with contentment and fell asleep. No bird cry ever disturbed him. The bushland and the swampland were very wonderful places.

Chapter V
THE TRAPPERS

ALONG the creek, about half a mile from the old bark hut, there was a rather deep pool in which lurked fat perch, and when old Bob felt like a change from damper and corned meat, he would take his rod and line and angle for these fish. Sometimes he would sit for hours on end placidly smoking his pipe while the fish refused to respond to the lure of the enticing worm or cricket dangling from the hook. But the swaggie had lots of time and patience.

If he caught a fish, he was happy; if he came away without any, he did not care. He left the hut one mid-morning carrying his rod and marched along the track that followed the creek right down to the swamps. Around him as he walked he was aware of the bush's manifold voices as his "children" went about their daily tasks. It seemed to him that he alone was on holiday.

He smiled with joy as a flock of little finches swept across the track right in front of him. They were red-browed firetails, or, as Bob called them, "red-heads." The bush was always filled with them and their merry whistles.

As he rounded a bend in the track he caught sight of an object on the ground that made him frown with annoyance. It was a bird trap, of wood and wire, placed under a small bush, and both its doors were set. In the middle compartment was a redhead, hopping about and whistling and, unknown to itself, acting as a decoy or "caller" for its wild bush kinsfolk.

The swagman looked around him, but could detect no human interlopers. He guessed readily that the trap had been set by boys, and those boys would be in the vicinity, probably crouched behind a convenient bush watching the trap, around which, on the ground, bird seed had been scattered. The bush birds, attracted by the "caller's" whistling, would fly into the low bush, see the seed and drop down to the trap to eat. A twig set in the trap held back the spring door, and if any hungry little bird tried to perch on the twig, the door would fall and it would be a prisoner.

Old Bob stood over the trap for a moment, looking down on the decoy. Then he glanced around. It appeared that he had the bush to himself. The owners of the trap had probably grown tired of watching it and had wandered off somewhere. Perhaps they had other traps set along the creek and were visiting them in turn. The old man's first impulse was to break the trap into small pieces, but he resisted the temptation.

Dropping to his haunches, he made seductive noises at the imprisoned redhead, which was busily eating seed from the bottom of the trap. Then he calmly pulled two wires from the middle compartment and stood up. The little "caller" soon perceived the way to freedom and in a flash was through the gap and away into the scrub. Old Bob watched it go with satisfaction and was turning to resume his journey to the fishing pool, when two boys appeared on the path, one carrying a trap similar to that on the ground.

As they approached, the swagman eyed them with dislike. One boy was a loutish looking individual, aged about 14. The other was conspicuous for his well-patched trousers. He was a year or two younger.

Both boys were without hats and each was badly in need of a haircut. Taking them all in all, they were an unattractive couple.

Catching sight of the old man standing over the trap, they came to a halt about fifty yards away and eyed him uncertainly.

"Good day, mate," said the elder, who was carrying the trap. Bob saw that it contained several spotted-sided finches or diamond sparrows.

"What have you fellers got in that there trap?" demanded Bob, not troubling to answer the greeting.

"Three wedge-tailed eagles and six wild swans," grinned the younger boy. "What do you want to know for, anyway, old timer?"

"None of your lip, youngster," grunted old Bob. "You've been trapping birds, diamond sparrows by the look of 'em. Well, just you let 'em go."

"Aw, don't be silly, mate," said the loutish youth. "We're goin' round sellin' these birds. We'll get three bob a pair for 'em."

"Yeh? That's what you think, young feller," said Bob. "Here, gimme that trap. What right have you to come here catching birds to sell?"

"I think this old joker's a bit mad, Fred," said the loutish youth to his companion. Suddenly he broke off and gave a shout.

"Hey, where 'as our redhead caller got to?"

"If you mean that little bird that was in this trap here, I let him go," said Bob. "Yes, let him go, same as I'm going to let those diamond sparrows go."

The loutish youth gave a roar of anger.

"Why, you old tramp, I'll knock your 'ead off for that," he howled. "Fred, you 'old this trap. I'm gonna 'ave a piece of this old coot."

Old Bob's eyes gleamed as the loutish youth walked up to him belligerently. He did not know if the youth intended to attack him, but he did know that as soon as the youth got close enough, he was going to grab him and box his ears soundly. That would teach him to trap birds along this creek.

"Knock him down and jump on him, Bert," called the youth, Fred, to his loutish companion. "You won't need my 'elp."

Bert advanced to within striking distance of the swagman, clenched his fist and drew back his arm for a punch. Then he gave a wild howl and lurched sideways as old Bob's open palm collided with his right ear with a sound like that of a pistol shot—or the last note of a coach-whip bird.

"Let that be a lesson to you, you young impudent devil," said Bob, as the youth, Bert, rubbed his tingling ear.

"You ain't gonna let 'im get away with that, are you, Bert?" called out Fred from a safe distance. "Kick 'im in the shins."

Bert, who had no boots on, discarded that idea, probably thinking that his toes and not the swagman's bony shin, would suffer the most. He continued to rub his ear and glare at old Bob, who glared back.

"Wot did you want to let out our redhead for?" demanded Fred. "You don't own this bush, you old coot."

"That will be enough from you, too, young feller-me-lad," said Bob. "None of your cheek, or you'll get a bit of what I just gave your mate here. The both of you would do much better if you went home and had a good wash and then got your hair cut. You look like a pair of retriever dogs."

Fred and Bert both thought that over for a moment and then they held a conference while old Bob stood by the trap and watched them closely. He guessed they were cooking up something against him, and he was correct.

"Let's rush him together," counselled Bert. "I'll go for him bull-headed, while you get round the back and tackle him from behind."

"Good-oh. When you say the word," agreed Fred.

"Right!" exclaimed Bert, and they rushed upon old Bob, Fred running in a circle to come upon him from the rear, while Bert, his head down, charged like a bull. Old Bob appreciated the plan and just as Bert got to within a few feet of him, he leapt lightly aside. Bert, his head still down, kept on going and met his friend Fred in exhilarating collision, his hard skull encountering Fred in the pit of the stomach. Fred gave a howl of anguish and fell over backwards, Bert sprawling on top of him.

Leaving them to sort themselves out, the swagman hurried over to where the trap containing the diamond sparrows lay in the grass. Deftly he opened the side door and in a few seconds the five birds were among their native trees.

With two howls of complete rage, Bert and Fred, who had dragged themselves to their feet again, made a rush at the old man. He faced them like an outraged lion and succeeded in administering a stinging smack to Fred's cheek before they grabbed him.

The old swaggie, with two lusty youths clinging to him, hitting and kicking, might have suffered some damage had not assistance come. In the excitement of the moment, none of them heard the quick barking of a dog, but the presence of the animal was forced home upon Fred of the well-patched pants, when he felt an insistent tugging from the rear. A hasty glance over his shoulder told him that a black kelpie dog had attached itself to one of the patches.

It was Roddy's dog, Tiger, and Tiger was thinking that at last he was embarking on his Great Adventure. He did not know what it was all about, except that two youths were attacking his friend, old Bob.

With Tiger hanging to the seat of his pants, Fred was not now of much assistance to his loutish mate, Bert, who was receiving a severe buffeting from the angry swagman.

Then, from among the trees, came a shout, and another antagonist joined in the fray. It was Roddy himself. He had been out for a run with Tiger, and when the dog suddenly had dashed away with excited barks, the lad had followed him quickly, because Tiger was a dog who deliberately went looking for trouble and generally managed to find it. Life was never dull with Tiger around.

Roddy, bursting through the trees on to the creek track, was horrified to see his old friend Bob being attacked by two over-grown boys. He did not stop to inquire what the trouble was, but sailed into the fray. Roddy was, normally, a gentle-souled boy, and definitely not the rowdy type; but he was no coward, and the sight of two youngsters attacking an old man like Bob filled him with a great rage and a deep disgust.

Just as he reached the scene of combat, Tiger withdrew from it—with a large piece of material in his mouth. The boy Fred, the seat of his trousers now completely gone, was in no mood for battle. As Tiger disappeared up the path, alternately dropping the cloth and picking it up again, Fred rushed into the dense thickets and was lost to view.

Roddy seized Bert round the waist and with a strong pull managed to get him away from old Bob. He swung the loutish youth around and his eyes blazed.

"What do you think you are doing, Bert Baker?" he demanded. "How dare you fight an old man like Bob? You should be ashamed of yourself, you coward!"

"The old coot let our birds out of our traps," roared Bert. "I'm gonna kill 'im!"

"If you want to kill somebody, try me," invited Roddy. "I'm nearer to your age."

"Don't interfere, Roddy, or you might get hurt. He's much older and bigger than you," said old Bob anxiously. "I'm not hurt, son. It would take more than that pair of retriever dogs to mark me."

"I'm not afraid of Bert Baker, the big bully," said Roddy and punched the loutish youth on the chin. Bert gave a sharp howl and made a whack at Roddy, but missed. Roddy followed up the first blow with another, a punch which landed right in Bert's left eye.

And, while Bert was hopping around and moaning, his hands clasped to his eye which was rapidly assuming a darkish hue, Tiger, hurrying back from the spot where he had dug a hole and buried the seat of Fred's pants, galloped around the loutish youth three times and then seized him by his dilapidated trousers.

In spite of their anger, the ludicrous sight was too much for Roddy and old Bob. They both burst into loud laughter as Bert, holding his eye with one hand, tried to beat off the dog with the other. Tiger, however, was a tenacious animal, and his one aim in life now was to collect the seat of this youth's trousers and add it to Fred's in the hole under the log up near Bob's hut.

Roddy, choking with laughter, called on Tiger to desist, but Tiger didn't hear his young master. This might not be the Great Adventure, but it was something very much like it, and the dog intended to make the most of it.

There came, suddenly, an ominous ripping sound, followed by a loud howl as if Tiger, in securing the trousers cloth, had, inadvertently, secured a little piece of Bert also. The black kelpie dropped the rag on the grass, gave a short bark of exultation, picked it up again, and dashed off toward the old bark hut.

The loutish youth, ignoring Roddy and old Bob whose faces were purple with laughter, picked up both empty bird traps and limped away through the trees, muttering nasty things under his breath.

"Oh, gosh! I've never laughed so much since old Peter

Jackson tried to ride a log across the Murrumbidgee River and had to swim because it was too small for him," said old Bob. "What a day! I was wild with those young fellers for trapping birds, and they had no right to hit an old man like me, but it has ended so funny that I forgive them both."

"Yes, it was funny," agreed Roddy with a grin, "but that doesn't excuse those two from attacking you, Bob. You wait until I meet Bert Baker again. Just you wait."

"Now, now, young feller-me-lad, don't be so bloodthirsty. All's well that ends well," said the swagman.

And, some hundreds of yards away, in a little clearing, Tiger, the kelpie, was carefully placing a tattered piece of cloth in a hole preparatory to covering it with earth. He had deemed it wiser not to hide it with the other piece under the log.

Then, having scratched the last pawful of earth over his treasure, he barked in triumph, and scampered back to join his young master.

Chapter VI
THE BLUE WREN'S GUEST

ON the higher twigs of a thick bush that was shut away by tall trees, two blue wrens whistled and played about, filled with the very joy of living. The sunlight sparkled on bush and scrub, the air was clear and the sky was blue—conditions enough to make any little bird joyful.

But there were greater, more personal reasons why little Bluecap and his mate should be so happy. They had finished their nest and soon would be family-raising. The home of their future brood swung in the air between small branches suspended from twigs, yet prevented from swaying about too much by clever stays of grass and hair woven by the birds into strong string. It was not only a triumph of bird architecture, but of engineering skill. Little wonder, then, that the small builders rejoiced.

The entrance to the nest was very small, only large enough for the wee birds themselves to enter. The inside was cosily lined with feathers and woolly materials picked up in various places. Soon there would be three or four eggs in it, and then would come the serious business of hatching.

Bluecap was a jaunty little chap with dainty and engaging ways. His song was a rollicking one and he was beautiful to look upon. Not so his rather drab little brown mate. Bluecap, however, considered that he made up for any shortcomings as to looks in the family.

In their little home-made bush haven, it seemed as if they would be quite safe from intrusion. They had no fear of either Old Bob or Roddy. These humans were their friends.

One morning, about two weeks after the nest had been completed, Roddy was lying in bed half-asleep, trying to make up his mind to get up and bring in the cows for milking. Shortly he would hear his father's voice, telling him that that job had to be done, and he was debating in his boyish mind whether he should await the call or arise now, when he heard a different sort of call. It was the note of a bird, a new one in old Bob's sanctuary, yet one that the lad had heard before. Bronze-back, the cuckoo, had returned.

Roddy was out of bed in a twinkling and, having dressed hurriedly, went outside. Once again he heard the cuckoo's call. It seemed as if the singer's sweet tones ran up in a scale of semitones, but Roddy could never be certain of that, or whether it was just the same note repeated. Old Bob always said it was all one note.

It was not yet time for him to bring in the cows, so he hurried along the bush track in the hope of seeing the cuckoo. He kept his eyes wide open, but could not locate the bird, try as he would. He returned to the farmhouse disappointed, but resolving to have another look that afternoon. This time he was successful. He came upon the visitor perched on the branch of a tree not far from Bluecap's nest.

The visitor showed her splendid plumage in the

sunlight, a blaze of bronze-green, shining with metallic lustre, and barred across the breast in white and brown. A bold, arrogant bird, she sat on the branch with a far-away look in her eyes as if she were interested in matters at a distance and had no knowledge or care of affairs close to hand.

That, of course, was merely her pose, because she was quite alive to what was going on around her. Her arrival in old Bob's sanctuary had caused tremendous excitement and aversion, something approaching what humans might feel if a burglar, armed with pistol, came uninvited to a festive party.

Witloo, the diamond sparrow, Willie Wagtail, little Jacky Winter, Bob the flycatcher, Bluecap and his mate, and all the little finches, redheads, zebras, blood-birds and others, whistled and fluttered in anxiety. Ping, the stockwhip bird cracked his whip, Long Bill, the honeyeater dashed wildly about, and Slow Wings, the peewit, flapped around and screamed his flat-toned call.

But the wildest and most anxious of them all was Bluecap and his little mate. Something seemed to tell them that Bronze-back had a particular interest in their nest.

After a while, taken aback a little by the combined demonstration of hostility, the cuckoo flew away, many of the small birds chasing her and twittering insults. Next day, however, she was back again. Day after day, Roddy haunted the place looking for her, and day after day, Bronze-back haunted the place, too; for she had decided that Bluecap's nest would suit her purpose admirably.

Hidden in the bushes, Roddy kept his eyes glued on the cuckoo. With a flock of small birds around her, whistling and chattering and making feint attacks, she flew to the ground not far away from where the boy was hidden. Roddy was thrilled, because never before had he seen a cuckoo at such close quarters. As he watched breathlessly, he saw her lay a large egg on the grass. Carefully she picked it up in her bill and flew slowly towards Bluecap's nest, the flock of protesting little birds still around her.

Ignoring them, the cuckoo reached the wrens' nest and, with strong wings holding her practically stationary outside the side entrance, she deftly slipped her egg into it. It lay on top of four smaller eggs from which Bluecap and his mate hoped four baby wrens would be hatched. Then, having carried out what she considered were her complete maternal duties, the cuckoo was away in a flash like a streak of flying copper. Nobody would see her near the nest again. No longer was she interested in her egg. Other birds would hatch it for her and feed the lusty chick.

All the little birds were overjoyed to see the last of the bronze cuckoo. As to her egg, that remained in the nest and the little wrens covered it with their warm feathers as if it were their own.

One day the eggs began to hatch and presently there were three baby wrens in the nest. The fourth egg was worthless and was thrown out by the birds. At once there began a busy feeding round for the parents, both doing their utmost to satisfy the hungry cravings of their children.

Just a week after the last wren's egg had been hatched, the big cuckoo egg cracked and a large chick sprawled out, roughly pushing the wren nestlings out of the way.

And what excitement followed! The advent of the cuckoo chick was the signal for another gathering of all the little birds, many of whom joined Bluecap and his mate in helping to feed the ravenous creature. Young bronze-back grew apace and soon the nest was not large enough to hold the four nestlings. That did not worry the interloper. He just rubbed and wriggled until he succeeded in getting each of them on to his back and, one by one, he pushed them from the nest to fall helplessly to the ground. It was not very long before the wren's nest was too small to contain him, so he moved out of it on to a perch nearby. And there he sat, an ungainly, fluffy ball, while Bluecap, his mate and half a dozen other little birds were run off their legs and wings supplying him with food. No matter how hard they worked, he still squawked for more.

In the manner of his kind, he grew rapidly, feathers developed and soon he was making short tumbling flights. These took him nowhere, but he always managed to land on a branch, where the bush's willing slaves still fed him. Perhaps they wanted him to grow quickly so that he would leave them.

In due course, some of the glossy lustre of his mother began to show in his plumage. Each day it became brighter and he became bigger until the moment arrived when Bluecap and his friends decided to have nothing further to do with the awkward-looking thing. They ceased feeding him and, in shrill voices, told him to clear out and never return to those parts again. He did not understand them at first, but squawked for food. He didn't get any. Clouds of little birds came from all parts of old Bob's sanctuary, flew around him, dashed in his face and shrilled and squeaked, telling him as plainly as they could that he had outworn his welcome.

Suddenly he went. A shaft of golden light came through the trees and chanced to fall on the bronze plumage of the departing and unwelcome guest. It seemed as though he went in a blaze of glory and Roddy, as well as all the little birds, was glad to see the last of him. The boy hoped that now the wrens would be able to raise another family of their own.

Almost every day he visited their little haven. If they chanced to be away, he peeped into the nest, without touching it. Then one day he saw four eggs lying there snugly. The nest had been cleaned out and re-lined and it looked very cosy. The boy prayed that the weather would remain fine so that Bluecap and his mate would have every chance to raise their family.

And the Weather God was kind; for, a few weeks after he had seen the four fledglings in the nest, they came to visit him at the farm—six little birds, four smaller than the other two. They were Mr. and Mrs. Bluecap and their four children, hopping merrily about on the lawn in front of the house and chirping to each other.

It was as if they had come to tell him that they had completely forgotten their unwelcome foster son, the bronze cuckoo.

Chapter VII
SLOW WINGS, THE PEEWIT

THE shrill notes of Slow Wings, the peewit, and his mate, were very familiar sounds both in old Bob's sanctuary and around Roddy's farm home. From earliest dawn, when Slow Wings called sweetly, "Bob-o-link! Bob-o-link!" until Jack Kookaburra laughed down the curtain of night, the varied calls of the peewits were heard. Slow Wings was not always a sweet singer. He was capable of uttering harsh, unattractive notes.

But when they were nesting, sometimes there were periods of blessed silence. Nesting time is always a busy period for any birds. Slow Wings and his mate were masons, constructing their large nest shaped like a pudding basin, out of mud, reinforced with straw and feathers and other binding material. Most of Slow Wings relations favored the bare limbs of trees that jutted over water as nesting sites, but Slow Wings and his mate selected a very tall gum tree near the creek.

"That bird has more names than a burglar," old Bob said to Roddy one day as they watched Slow Wings carrying mud from the creek bank to the nest. "Most bad men who break the law have a string of names. Some people call peewits mudlarks because they make their nests out of mud. Others call them magpie larks, peewees,

53

Murray magpies, little magpies, pugwalls, and other names, too."

No matter what name Slow Wings went under, he and his kind were welcome visitors to the farm, for their meals were entirely of insects, worms, slugs and other such items. The most tempting crops of fruit or grain could not make them become vegetarians. One favorite dish of Slow Wings was fat spiders—the fatter the better. The birds, too, loved green places and were never far away from water. They liked to patrol creek banks and pick up water creatures.

Ploughing time on the farm was a most agreeable period for the peewits, because it meant plenty of fat grubs turned up by the ploughshares. Often they had to compete with their larger counterparts, the magpies, and sometimes with other birds, but Slow Wings always got his share. So quick was he in connecting ploughing with fat grubs that when he saw the horses being driven out to the plough, he was flying around, his beak watering in anticipation, and his flat voice never quiet. Though he flew around in a seemingly slow and weak fashion, his wings were sturdy and strong, capable of carrying him long distances should the occasion demand it.

Roddy liked to watch the peewit playing about or collecting food and building materials. He admired the graceful little black-and-white birds, so like his big brother, the magpie, and yet so different. On his thin legs he looked fragile, but he was far from being a delicate bird; neither was he a timid one. Lacking the vicious pugnacity of the magpie, he still could give a good account of himself when the odds were even, and he was not a bird to shrink from either hard working or hard fighting.

It was a very tall tree in which the peewits had built their big mud nest, and the nest was occupied by four large blotched eggs, the pride of their hearts. The birds were fairly safe from attack by ground enemies, even small boys, for the mud home was not on a limb strong enough to support the weight of an ordinary-sized lad. Owls and hawks, too, would find attack difficult because the foliage was thick around the nest.

But there were other enemies.

One day, Slow Wings returned home hurriedly from foraging, to find his mate in a state of excitement, directing a stream of insults at a small goanna, about two feet long, that had climbed the tree trunk and was now on the limb and within a few feet of the nest itself. Mrs. Slow Wings was sitting on the nest and intended to stay there until the last moment. She had no intention of giving up her eggs without a life-and-death struggle.

Slow Wings had heard his mate's shrill cries of distress while he had been hunting along the swamp's edge and he had come hurrying home. With a screech of rage he flew at the intruder, beating its ugly head with his wings and bringing beak and claws into action.

The goanna was only a small one, but that did not lessen its danger. Slow Wings made little impression upon its heavily-armored head, but did distract its attention from the nest. Then Mrs. Slow Wings joined in, her heart beating wildly inside her. The goanna was now hard-pressed to defend his eyes from the twin beaks, thin and sharp, and he decided that the nest was not worth worrying about. Turning tail, he scuttled down the tree trunk to the ground, with Slow Wings circling round and screeching. His mate returned to the nest. Danger was not pressing now, and it was most important that the eggs be kept warm.

When the goanna reached the ground Slow Wings tackled it again. It scuttled round the trunk as if to climb the tree a second time and the peewit prepared to try to prevent it.

Suddenly a loud laugh made the bird's heart leap with joy. Jack Kookaburra was in a nearby tree and was watching the contest. His laugh, however, was not one of amusement at the peewit's dilemma. It was the battle cry of a kookaburra prepared to attack.

Again the big bird laughed. This time it was a warning to Slow Wings to get out of the way and allow a bird, whose business was reptile-killing, enough space to do battle. Slow Wings whirled aloft to the nest branch and as he did so, Jack Kookaburra launched himself straight at the goanna, which was now a few feet up the tree trunk.

Like an arrow from a bow, the grey bird, huge pointed beak stretched straight in front of him, flew at that goanna, and, with unerring aim, drove his death-dealing weapon into the back of the reptile's neck. The thing fell kicking to earth and the kookaburra, picking it up with his strong bill, bashed it heavily against the tree trunk. Then, the goanna firmly held in his beak, he rose slowly and heavily from the ground under the weight of what he intended to be a hearty meal. Slow Wings watched him as, with some difficulty, he flew away to the tall tree from which, in his own exalted opinion, he directed the affairs of the bird world. His mate joined him there and helped him to dispose of the goanna.

One day a remarkable adventure befell Slow Wings. He was scouting round the farm seeing what he could collect in the way of food, when a motor car arrived. It was Roddy's uncle George from the city, paying a visit, but Slow Wings didn't know that. He wouldn't have cared, anyway. He was not very interested in human beings as such; but he was interested in this motor car. He had never seen anything like it before.

From the top of a tree he listened to the throbbing of the engine and after it had stopped and there were no human beings in sight, he decided to inspect the strange object. He flew down from the tree and alighted on the car roof. He ran around this for a few moments and then dropped down on the open window edge. Peering inside, he saw, protruding from a worn part of the upholstery, some strands of fibre which might make good nest-repairing material. Hopping on to the seat, he pulled some of the stuff out with his strong beak and, having tested the strength, decided to take it away.

As he was preparing to leave, he glanced towards the windscreen and saw what he took to be another peewit glaring at him. He was annoyed to think that this strange bird might steal the fibre. The only thing to do was to put the stranger to flight Slow Wings flew at his reflection in the glass and got a shock when his beak hit the hard material and he was sent sprawling back on to the car seat.

But he was a fighter and attacked again and again. No matter where he flew, that other bird was always there, facing him.

This fighting in an enclosed place made no appeal to him. He decided to give battle in the open so, darting out of the window, he flew round the windscreen to attack the interloper. No bird was there, but when he looked into the glass, he discovered that his visitor was inside the car.

Very much annoyed, Slow Wings flew round and into the car again, screeching defiance. He made such a noise that Roddy, who was working at the back of the farmhouse, came along to see what the trouble was. What he saw made him laugh heartily.

This laughter made Slow Wings wake up to himself. He didn't want to be trapped in the car by that boy, though he should have known from past experience that Roddy was his friend.

With a last dash at his "enemy" he fled to the top of the tall gum tree behind the cowsheds, from the heights of which he screeched a challenge to the mysterious peewit in the car to come out and fight.

Roddy was screaming with laughter, and when Jack Kookaburra perched on a branch of a tree a quarter of a mile away, joined in the fun with a mocking laugh, which echoed across the farmlands, Slow Wings realised that he was the target for their mirth.

So, with as much dignity as he could muster in the circumstances, he flapped away towards the swamps, hoping, in quiet places, to rid himself of the memories of motor cars, mysterious enemies and mocking boys and kookaburras.

Chapter VIII
OLD JIM CROW

VERY early, in the grey light of the morning, Roddy would hear Jack Kookaburra's laugh, waking the sleeping world, and almost immediately after would sound the melancholy voice of Jim Crow, like some sick child crying for a lost parent: "Father—fa-a-a-ther!"

Jim Crow, with his sober, black plumage and wicked white eyes, was the bush undertaker of old Bob's sanctuary, and he and his friends were out at the first flush of dawn, winging heavily across the sky to some feeding place among newly-planted grain, or where they might chance upon some dead thing.

Roddy did not like crows. He knew that they did some good by eating grasshoppers, beetles, cutworms and other destructive insects, but he could never forgive their habit of picking the eyes out of weak, new-born lambs and dying sheep He frowned also upon the crows for their raids upon the nests of other birds, stealing and eating their eggs and young ones.

When the feathered ink-spots left the tall trees in which they roosted over-night, they generally scattered, flying high, unless they knew of food close at hand. But high as they flew, little escaped their keen eyes. They quartered the ground, each bird prospecting a certain area, and as soon as it sighted something attractive, called to its mates.

If Jim Crow saw a dead or dying sheep, he swooped down at once and by the time he had reached the side of his potential meal, from all parts of the upper air his comrades who had seen him drop, came floating in like so many black snowflakes, all uttering their plaintive cry, "Father! Fa-a-a-ther!"

But Jim Crow wasn't their father—not the father of them all, anyway, even though he was very old and very wise.

It was seed time. The ground had been ploughed and the corn sown. Roddy's father had erected several scarecrows by the light of the moon on the previous night, and Boobook the owl, who had seen him doing it, wondered what on earth the mad human could be about. The scarecrows were pieces of wood in the shape of a man. They had round bags stuffed with grass for heads with an old hat perched on top, and each wore a tattered coat. They looked weird to the owl as he returned from his hunt, and in the dim dawnlight, looked even stranger.

But they held no terrors for old Jim Crow.

As Roddy was driving in the cows with the assistance of Tiger, he heard the dismal karking, far away at first, but coming steadily closer. Jim Crow, who ate almost any kind of food that he could get his claws on, had a particular passion for corn and other seed newly sown. Now he was leading his sable cohorts to the feast.

And Roddy's father had expected that this was what the black pests would do. That was why he had erected the scarecrows. But, knowing the cunning of the birds, he did not intend to trust to the efficiency of the scarecrows alone. So, before Roddy retired for the night, his father told him to get up early and lend reality to the deception by becoming a lively scarecrow himself.

The lad hurried the cows to the milking sheds, and while the family and the farm hands were attending to them, he went to the shed where he kept his rifle. With the loaded weapon in his hand and some spare cartridges in his pocket, he made for the cornfield. This was one of the rare occasions on which a gun, with justice, might be turned upon an inhabitant of old Bob's sanctuary.

As he neared the field, Roddy could see the crows still circling uncertainly above the high trees. They were nervous about the scarecrows, though old Jim was flapping around and karking out that the things were harmless. But still they hesitated, some of them settling among the trees to await developments.

Annoyed with his timid companions and determined to show them what fools they were, Jim Crow ceased circling around the trees and set off, winging slowly on a wide and craftily-chosen course which, to those who did not know him, seemed to be leading anywhere but to the cornfield. After him—a long way after, too—came a few of the bolder crows who had faith in their wise old leader. Roddy placed the rifle on the ground and climbed up on the fence, watching the birds' manoeuvre.

Slow Wings the peewit was very busy in the gums around the paddock, Willie Wagtail chattered and flirted among the cows, occasionally grabbing some pieces of hair from their backs, and the lovely carolling of Maggie the magpie was sweet on the morning air. But still old Jim

Crow flew, circling wide, with his black companions getting closer to him.

Roddy had intended watching them closely, but, boy-like, he allowed his attention to wander to a dozen other interesting things in the bird world. Then, when his thoughts came back to the job in hand, he saw Jim Crow sitting on the hat of a scarecrow, while his black mates were scattered over the tilled land, busily unearthing grain and gobbling it down.

Jim Crow was watching Roddy intently. He knew the boy had a gun with him. The old bird had had his experiences in the course of a long life—so he watched.

Climbing stealthily down from his seat on the fence, the boy made a quick grab at the rifle. But before he could aim and fire it, Jim called loudly: "Karr! karr!"

Immediately, a black cloud rose from the cornfield and the bullet from the gun hit the old hat upon which Jim had been sitting. As he circled overhead, the old bird karked derisively, "Fa-arther!"

Boldly he dropped again, this time to the earth and began to prospect for grain. In his experience, which was a crowded one, he had never heard a gun go off twice near that farm without an interval between the shots—time for the reloading. So down dropped all his friends; that is, all except one, who took up his position on the scarecrow's hat.

Roddy reloaded the rifle, but did not fire it. He had decided to try a little strategy himself. Away he strolled, down towards the creek. He wanted Jim Crow to believe that he had lost interest in the field and that the crows could eat all the corn they desired. When he reached the creek, he stole around through the scrub to a point opposite that in which he had stood to fire the first shot. He at length approached the field under cover of some tea-tree and, peering through the twigs and leaves, saw that all the crows, including old Jim and the former sentry, were feeding on the ground.

As he stepped carefully so that no crackling twigs would warn the thieves, the idea that he must kill old Jim as the ringleader in these depredations, took complete possession of Roddy's mind. From stump to stump he dodged, holding the rifle behind him. He did not want his quarry to get the slightest inkling of his presence and the sun glinting on the weapon could easily give the show away. As it was, he expected, every moment, to hear Jim Crow's warning "kark" and to see the black flock disperse rapidly.

At length the boy reached a vantage spot where the crows could not see him but he could observe their every movement. There they were, scattered all over the earth, eating voraciously. There must have been thirty of them.

Patiently the lad waited. He wanted a good shot at Jim. But that bird was hard to get in the sights of the rifle. Roddy raised the weapon and took aim. Old Jim stopped eating, raised his black head and glanced around. He was uneasy, but could see nothing to disturb him. He had, however, an amazing instinct for danger. Something was wrong, and he knew it. He flew to the scarecrow and, perched on the old hat, glared around, his white eyes wary and alert.

It was a first class target for the bush boy, and Roddy was an excellent shot. Slowly bringing the rifle to his shoulder, he pressed the trigger.

And as he did so, a wave of compassion for Jim Crow came over him. Too late! Yes, for, as the gun roared, old Jim dropped like a stone. A whirring of wings and wild "karks" came from the terrified flock as Roddy rushed over the rough earth. They whirled off into the sky and made for the horizon with all the speed of which they were capable.

Roddy heard them in a dream. This couldn't be true, he told himself. Old Jim Crow dead. Why hadn't he fired at some other bird? Jim had been too bold, too brave, sitting on the scarecrow to warn the others. Why, had it not been for him, they never would have had their feast of corn. They had all been too cowardly to drop to earth until brave old Jim had shown them the way.

The boy's heart was in his throat, pounding and pumping, as he knelt over the stricken bird.

"I'm sorry, Jim Crow," he said in a whisper. "Poor old Jim Crow—I'm sorry, truly I am."

The old bird's eyes were shut, but as the lad spoke, the black lid lifted from one white-rimmed eye, then closed again. It was as if old Jim had winked; as if he said, "All right, my son. You got me that time. You were too clever for old Jim Crow."

With tears in his own eyes, Roddy turned his head away. He could not bear to look upon the stricken bird. He would have to bury it, he told himself, and what was more fitting place than in the middle of the cornfield. He would dig a grave immediately.

Slowly he turned to pick up the poor old bird. But Jim Crow wasn't there. In amazement, Roddy looked quickly around. There was no sign of Jim.

The lad stood up. And then he saw Jim Crow—sitting on the scarecrow's hat and looking at him. Deliberately, it seemed to Roddy, the bird winked.

"Good gracious," said the boy. "The bullet must have only grazed him and stunned him for a moment!"

Stooping down, he picked up a clod of dirt, intending to toss it at the sly old bird. When he straightened up, however, Jim wasn't on the scarecrow. He was high in the air and, as he circled above the lad's head, he called out derisively,

"Fa-arther!"

Roddy shook his fist at Jim and laughed heartily.

Chapter IX
THE DIVE BOMBERS

RODDY had taken his sister to see the rock-warblers' nest in old Bob's hut. Susan loved the wild birds as much as Roddy did, but she did not possess the boy's patience. Whereas Roddy would be content to lie hidden in the one spot for an hour or more on the off-chance of seeing some favorite bird at work or play, Susan would spare neither the time nor the trouble.

Be that as it may, the birds trusted her as much as they trusted her brother; perhaps more. Old Bob had often stated that in all his wanderings he had learned, over and over again, that birds trusted girls more than boys.

Susan had duly inspected the rock-warblers' nest in the hut and had been delighted. It contained another brood, and old Bob had reported that, unlike the first occasion, there had been no nestlings thrown out—nor had any fallen out.

While Roddy and old Bob chatted away inside the hut, the little girl sat outside on an old bench doing some knitting she had brought with her. She was an industrious child.

Hearing a slight rustle in a nearby tree, she glanced up, to see a kookaburra sitting on a low branch.

"Hello, Jack!" she called softly. "Come down here to me."

The bird looked at her wisely, turning its head as if to see her better. It would not come any closer, however, and presently flew away. When Roddy came out of the hut soon afterwards, she mentioned the matter.

"It could not have been old Jack Kookaburra," said the boy. "I saw him down by the cornfield as we were coming here. Perhaps it was his mate."

"Tomorrow I'm going to bring some meat down here," said Susan. "If she comes again I'll try to feed her and make friends."

"What for?" asked old Bob, coming to the hut door.

"I'd like to see her eat out of my hand," said the girl.

"What for?" asked old Bob again.

"I think it would be nice and friendly," said Susan.

"Um, yes, I suppose it would," agreed the swagman. "But I don't think it would be wise to coax any kookaburras around this here hut while them there rock warblers are nesting. The kooka might take a fancy to them for a meal."

"Oh, I'd be careful to see that nothing like that happened," Susan assured him, and the old man grunted.

"Anyway, as I'm leaving at dawn for another trip down south, you two will be in charge of the hut. If that nest isn't there when I get back, I'll search out that kookaburra and wring it's neck," said old Bob darkly, while Roddy and his sister laughed at the idea of Bob hurting any bird.

On the following afternoon, accompanied by her brother, Susan went to the hut, and while the boy stayed inside out of sight, she waited patiently for the kookaburra to arrive. She did not have long to wait. The kookaburra flew on to the same branch as before and Susan threw a piece of meat on the ground under it. The wise bird looked at it for a time and then dropped lightly to investigate. Susan was delighted when the kookaburra seized the meat and flew off.

Roddy laughed when she repeated her desire to have the kookaburra tame enough to eat from her hand.

"It's no use trying to tame the wild things," he said. "I've tried it over and over again. Anyway, I don't believe in taming them. I like them better, free as the air."

"What you mean is that you can't do it," Susan retorted. "Birds are afraid of boys."

"Maybe. I think, though, that when birds are tamed they become too trusting and unwary. Then something gets them—a cat, another bird, or even a snake."

Susan, however, decided to persist with her little scheme, and day after day she went to the hut, and every day Jack Kookaburra's mate came there, too, and was given a piece of nice raw meat. Gradually the girl succeeded in enticing the bird right down to an old chair which she had set outside. Lady Kookburra actually sat on the back of this chair and accepted meat from the girl's hand.

Roddy was as delighted as his sister when he first witnessed the jolly sight, but he struck a note of warning.

"Just you wait until the tree martins come back," he said. "Their nest is up in a hollow branch of that white gum. They have been nesting there for years, and when they find that a kookaburra makes a habit of coming around here, they'll go completely mad."

"If they dare to touch my kookaburra, I'll go home and get your rifle," Susan said determinedly.

Some weeks later, when Susan had trained her kookaburra to go right inside the old hut and take food from her as she sat at the table, she heard a chattering, scolding sound outside.

Going to the door, she saw two birds, not as large as a thrush but bigger than a finch, flying and chirping in the air around the hut. Blue-beak the martin and his mate had returned for the nesting season, and as Roddy had predicted, they objected strongly to the presence of a kookaburra. One of the little birds almost flew into the hut, but changed its mind, swerving away, chattering and scolding. The lady kookaburra ignored them completely for a time until, finding that there was no more free food from Susan, opened her wings and flew out to perch on top of a post near the hut door.

Her appearance was greeted with loud harsh cries by the two martins and the kookaburra hardly had time to fluff out her feathers before they both were on her. It was a marvellous exhibition of dive-bombing. One of the little birds soared into the air directly above the pole, wheeled and came down in a screaming power-dive, its beak making a grinding, gnashing sound. Right on to the kookaburra's head it dived, swerved slightly, yet giving the large bird a sharp rap as it passed. Blue-beak followed his mate in her pretty aerial manoeuvre, but this time, as he dropped, the wary kookaburra raised her long, sharp beak, causing the martin to swerve quickly. He knew full well what would happen to him if he hit that formidable weapon.

Time after time the small dive-bombers attacked, but

beyond raising her beak occasionally, the kookaburra took hardly any notice. Eventually, becoming tired of the din they were creating, she flew unhurriedly away.

This performance was repeated on several days in succession much to Susan's amusement.

One afternoon when the girl went to the hut she found the lady kookaburra awaiting her, but she was not alone. There, on the same branch was old Jack Kookaburra himself. Evidently, thought Susan, Mrs. Jack had told her husband all about the free feeds of meat she had been getting and he had thought that he might as well be in it, too.

But Jack was wary. When his mate went inside the hut, he remained out in the tree, watching anxiously and evidently fearing a trap. Jack was bigger than his mate and handsomer. There was more sheen on his plumage, and the wings and beak of this famous old fighter were longer than those of his more peaceful wife.

If Blue-beak and his mate had been indignant over the presence of one kookaburra, they were doubly angry about the advent of two. They discussed the matter excitedly in the tree top, wondering how they could get him to go away and take his wife with him. They did not feel inclined to attack this he might not feel like ignoring dive-bombing assaults. He might take direct action. The martins knew that kookaburras were killers of young birds, and of adult ones too, if they were small. Old Jack might often unwittingly protect his smaller brethren by killing the snakes that stole their eggs and nestlings, but if he chanced to be hungry and a nest of fledglings were near, he would lunch off them without a second thought.

And so the little tree martins were anxious about it all.

As it happened, they had no cause to worry for Jack had other things on his mind. While his mate was in the hut he had been making clucking noises and at length she yielded to his obvious desire that she should come out to him. Then, together the two kookaburras departed, much to the relief of the martins.

Coming out of the hut, Susan noticed with surprise and some dismay that Jack had not deigned to touch the raw meat she had placed on the ground for him. So she had been wrong in surmising that Jack had accompanied his mate so as to get a free feed. Then why had he troubled to come? Just for company?

Susan thought she had found the answer next day when neither of the kookaburras ventured near the hut; and the girl was sure that she had the correct answer when they did not show up after a whole week had passed.

"What do you think about it, Roddy?" she asked her brother.

"Well, I reckon that Jack Kooka came to warn her against traps," said the boy. "I think he thought you were trying to catch her."

"But I wouldn't do that," she protested.

"I know you wouldn't, but Jack Kookaburra doesn't," said Roddy. "He is suspicious of all human beings and likes to be on the safe side."

"You don't think he came just to spy out the martin's nest?" his sister asked, and there was anxiety in her tones.

"I shouldn't think so," Roddy told her.

"Perhaps she told him about the rock-warblers' nest in the hut. I often saw her looking up at it as she sat on the table eating food," said Susan. "I remember, too, that the rock-birds made a funny, chattering noise while she was there—just as if they were afraid of her."

"I have little doubt that they were afraid," said Roddy. "You may be right about the rock-birds. If I were you, I wouldn't take Mrs. Jacky into the hut again. Play safe."

"But how could she hurt them if I were there, too?" asked the girl. "And when I come out of the hut, I always close the door."

"Jack and his mate could easily get down the chimney."

"If Jack is so afraid of a trap, I don't think he'd come down the chimney," said Susan doubtfully.

"Probably not. The chimney might scare him. As a matter of fact, crows are trapped something like that. Farmers make a big wire cage and place a dead sheep in it. There is a hole at the top of the cage and when the crows enter, they can't get out. There is not enough room for them to fly and they cannot climb like parrots. They have to stay in the trap until the men come along with waddies and kill them."

"What cruel brutes some people are," exclaimed the girl. "No wonder the birds hate them. If anyone touches my kookaburras I'll kill them."

"Who is the cruel brute now?" laughed Roddy. "Why, Susan, you are really bloodthirsty!"

On the following day when the girl arrived at the hut, her indignation knew no bounds when she discovered both Jack Kookaburra and his mate trying to enter the place through the gap at the top of the door, while the two tree martins dive-bombed them relentlessly. Fortunately, the gap was far too small for the big birds, which, when they saw Susan, flew off and perched on their familiar branch.

"I'd like to know just why you two were trying to get into that hut," she said, looking at them.

"Were you looking for meat from me, or were you going to steal the little young ones from the rock birds' nest?"

Jack Kookaburra did the wrong thing—he laughed loudly.

Suddenly Susan felt very angry with him and his mate, regarding the latter as nothing but a deceiver and a hypocrite.

"Go away, both of you," she called out, waving her arms. "I don't ever want to see either of you again."

When Jack laughed again and his mate gave a hoarse chuckle of agreement, the angry girl ran under the branch and, clapping her hands, succeeded in putting them to flight. As they flew away, Bluebeak and his mate chattered a long farewell to them, and then chirped at Susan, telling her what a mistake she had been making in being friendly with such robbers and rogues as kookaburras.

As she opened the hut door to have a look at the rock-birds, Susan turned a kindly eye on the brave little tree-martins. Then one of them flew near as if trying to enter the hut.

"Shoo!" she called out loudly. "Go away. You can't have the rock-birds. Really, I don't know what to think about you birds. You all seem to want to eat one another's eggs and families. Not one of you may be trusted!"

Chapter X
THE HILLS OF HAPPINESS

A FLOCK of magpies lived in a line of gum trees on a distant ridge far to the east, which always caught the last rays of the setting sun and held them momentarily in a radiance of gold.

Roddy, an imaginative lad, with a tendency sometimes to poetry, called the ridge the Hills of Happiness. Anybody who passed the line of trees, especially at early morning or late evening, would be serenaded by the exhilarating music of many soft, warbling voices rising to sweet carolling. In the nesting season, the stranger ran the grave risk of being attacked viciously by the black-and-white songsters, for no bushland bird was more vicious and pugnacious in protecting his nest than Maggie the magpie and his kith and kin.

But, during the off-seasons, the pied songsters lived together sociably with no thought of attacking any-one. They had their own particular hunting grounds, each pair of birds to a given area, and they went about the serious business of living.

Roddy sometimes visited the Hills of Happiness, but never in the nesting season. He had no desire to disturb the magpies in their family-raising duties and he certainly had less desire to become the target for a sharp beak.

Magpies forgot their human friends at mating time and treated all the race as enemies.

"I like magpies," said old Bob one day. "They have everything a bird can have. They are brave, clever, first-class fighters, very useful in keeping down insect pests and have voices like opera singers. No wonder somebody once suggested that they should be called 'Anzac Birds.' They have just the spirit of the soldiers of the A.I.F."

It was the first time Roddy had heard old Bob actually praise a particular bird. The old man had so often told him that all the birds had their little faults and weaknesses. Apparently he thought magpies were perfect.

"They kill little birds at times," he said, to draw the old man out.

"They do. I admit it," said the swagman. "Not often though. There are bad eggs among them the same as among us people; but, like us people, most of them are honest-to-goodness first-class Australians."

Something in the old chap's tones made Roddy steal a sidelong glance at him. There was something almost grand, almost noble about old Bob—quite apart from his obvious kindness—that made Roddy think that he had not always been a wanderer. Possibly Bob liked wandering, lured on by the passionate desire to see new scenes, new faces and new episodes in life. But no matter where he wandered, the old man always came back to the old hut among his bush "children."

When Bob returned to his haven of beauty, he did his washing, mended his boots, darned his socks and patched any holes in his trousers, shirts or coat. He always stayed for several weeks, during which Roddy saw him as often as possible. He loved to sit and listen to the old man's stories of the track, the endless winding, wandering track, that went on and on, through bush or rich riverlands, where cool streams drifted down on their way to the sea. Sometimes his stories were of the vast, burning plains, where water was scarce and the living hard. But no matter the setting of the story, it was always alive, always vibrant, and the boy thrilled to the tale, proud to be living in such a glorious land as this, his own Australia.

A few days after his conversation with Bob, Roddy visited the hut one afternoon, and to his surprise found that the swagman had a guest—a very lively, squawking guest it was, too.

"A young magpie!" exclaimed the boy. "Where did you get it?"

"I took a walk this morning over on the far ridge, that place you call the Hills of Happiness," said Bob. "Hills of Hate, I'd call 'em, young feller. I've heard people say that nesting maggies only tackle small boys after their nests. Well, I'm no small boy, yet I got tackled to-day by a maggie. Vicious thing it was, too."

"This one?" inquired the boy.

"No. This feller is only a pup. Can't you see he hasn't got his full coloring yet? That grey will turn to black before he can say he is a man. Anyway, I found this young joker on the ground hobbling around. Got a broken leg, I guess. I'm going to mend it for him."

"How will you do that, Bob?" inquired Roddy.

"I've done what I can already, son. I've bound it up tight and I'm going to make this bird stay in a box until the leg is strong enough for him to get around on."

Roddy looked doubtful.

"I don't like your chances," he said. "How will you make him keep still?"

"Well, he can't fly yet, so shouldn't want to go gallivanting around the countryside," said the swaggie. "If he was at home he'd still be in the nest being fed by his dad and mother. I'm going to make a magpie's nest in this box and keep him in it. I'll keep him so well fed that he won't want to skip around."

"It might work," the boy said, slowly and thoughtfully.

"It'll work all right," Bob replied with complete confidence. "As long as this young joker gets his meals regular, he won't care a hoot who supplies them—me or his parents. You wait and see."

"Do you intend to keep him as a pet, Bob?"

"That's the thing that worries me, sonny boy," said the old man. "I don't believe in taming the wild things. Their proper place is among the trees. I'm afraid that he won't leave here when he's O.K. again. I don't mind him staying around the place, but I don't want him to be a tame pet. Anyway, who would look after him when I was away?"

"I would," said Roddy.

"I thought you'd say that, son," nodded Bob, "but if you fed him he'd hang around the place. We don't want him to become dependent on us for his tucker."

"Let's wait and see how things go on," said Roddy, and Bob said he guessed that that was all they could do.

As the days passed and merged into weeks, Bob's experiment proved a success. The old man had built a large nest of sticks and twigs in a butter box and had lined it with rags. The young magpie was quite at home and was perfectly happy as long as he was fed; and Bob saw that he was fed regularly. The swagman gave him pieces of raw meat, but not too much. The bird's main diet was worms, grubs and grasshoppers the swagman caught in the bush. His idea was to make the bird familiar with ordinary bush fare so that it could hunt for those delicacies when it returned to its native Hills of Happiness. For Bob was determined that the magpie should not become a tame pet around the hut.

The young magpie grew apace after the fashion of his race and the day at length arrived when he decided to leave the nest. His leg had long since mended, leading the swagman to believe that no bones had been broken at all.

"Dash me buttons, Bill," said old Bob, addressing the bird by the name he had given it, "I've spent too much time here looking after you. It's been months and I'm due to go away again on the track. I've got to work for my living, you know."

Bill squawked in sympathy and began to prospect the hut floor. He found nothing there to interest him, so hopped outside. Old Bob followed him. The bird poked his beak inquisitively into odd corners and then, turning to the swagman, squawked loudly.

"Hungry, eh? All right, Bill, dinner's coming up," said Bob and, taking several grasshoppers from a glass jar, threw them on the ground. They were still alive, but the sharp-eyed magpie made short work of them, hopping and pecking and gobbling like a veteran.

"You'll learn quick, Bill," exclaimed Bob in high delight. A sudden thought struck him. He caught the bird and carried it to the low branch of a tree on which he perched it. The branch was about five feet from the ground. Bill was surprised at the manoeuvre and gave a squawk of inquiry. Old Bob told him to get down the best way he could. Bill did—he fell down. Old Bob scratched his head.

"Hanged if I knew how I'm gonna teach you to fly, Bill," he muttered to himself. Bill hopped back to the hut doorway and Bob picked him up.

"This is a bit hard on you, mate, but it's got to be done," he said, and deliberately threw Bill high into the air. As the bird shot upwards, the swagman spread out his hands and stood ready to catch Bill if he tumbled. But Bill didn't tumble. Automatically he spread his wings and though he didn't fly, he volplaned to earth and landed gently.

"Good on yer, Bill!" ejaculated old Bob and went to pick the bird up for the third time. Bill, however, eluded his outstretched hands and deliberately, but awkwardly, flew to the low limb on which Bob first placed him.

"That will do me, cobber," said the swagman and, entering the hut, closed the door tightly so that the magpie could not get in again. He was not contemplating shutting Bill completely out of his life so soon, but he thought that if the bird were left to its own devices for a time, it might display some of that initiative so eminently possessed by all the magpie tribe.

He did not open the door again until a full hour had passed. Bill was nowhere in sight. The swagman scratched his head and wondered what could have become of him. He hoped that the bird had not yet gone away.

Bill hadn't. And Bob found that out suddenly when

his hat was knocked from his head and he found the magpie perched on his shoulder. Bill, in a spirit of adventure, had, after the door had been closed on him, made his way to the top of the tree and then had amused himself hopping from branch to branch.

When he saw old Bob come out he had, without thought, flown straight down intending to land on the ground in front of the old man. His aim, however, was not too good and he had hit the swagman on the head.

"Hey, Bill, cut that out!" exclaimed Bob, taking the bird from his shoulder and stroking its glossy plumage. "It's not nesting time yet. That's the time you fellers tackle people—when the eggs and young 'uns are in the nest!"

Saying which, he deftly tossed Bill high into the air. Bill spread his wings and flew to the low branch, where he sat and squawked complacently—quite pleased with himself and his flying lessons.

Roddy was greatly interested to hear the details when he called on Bob that night. Bill, scorning the nest, was sleeping on a rafter over their heads.

"I didn't like to leave him out all night so soon," said old Bob apologetically.

"You're spoiling him, Bob," chided the boy.

"Maybe, but not for long. I'm off on the track in a couple of days." He stopped, and looked sternly at the boy. "You see that you don't go spoiling him while I'm away, Roddy," he said. "He knows how to fly and I don't think he'll starve in the bush. When I go, you don't come near the hut for a couple of weeks. He'll soon forget us."

"I tell you what, Bob," said the boy. "On the day you

do leave, I'll take Bill over to the Hills of Happiness and let him go there. He'll join his friends, maybe his family, and he'll be all right."

"You've hit it, mate," said Bob. "Do that."

And Roddy did. He said farewell to Bob, whose track lay in the opposite direction and then, with Bill in his hands, the boy set off on his rather long walk. When he reached the line of trees on the ridge, he saw, on the grassland below, a flock of magpies spread out over the countryside, all busy getting their breakfasts. He walked as close as he could to them without causing them to fly and gently placed Bill on the ground. Bill saw his kith and kin and hurried off to join them. They took no notice of his arrival but went on hunting for grasshoppers, crickets and grubs.

Quite satisfied, Roddy turned homewards. Both he and old Bob had done their duty.

It was with some disgust that the lad, late that afternoon, found Bill back at the hut. The boy had been searching for a straying cow. He had no intention of entering the hut and was passing it by when he was greeted by a loud squawk. There sat Bill on his favorite low branch. Whether the other magpies had hunted him away, or whether he was homesick for old Bob, the boy could not guess. Surely Bill wasn't going to become a problem child? He was almost full grown and big enough and old enough to fiend for himself. Roddy felt a little annoyed with Bill.

"Well, I don't know, Bill," he said to the bird after some thought, "perhaps I can't blame you for liking old

Bob and wanting his company. Aren't we all the same? Still, I'm not going to mollycoddle you. You can sleep to-night in the trees, see?"

He walked on without a backward glance and Bill watched him go with no desire to follow him. Bill liked Roddy, but not enough to chum up with him.

Old Bob was his favorite. Bill loved the old man, and wanted to see him again. He did not realise that old Bob would not be in those parts for many weeks to come.

In the days and weeks that passed, Roddy was often near the hut and on most occasions he saw Bill. He wondered how the bird was getting on, but did not try to make friends with it. He was sticking to his determination not to mollycoddle it.

As a matter of fact, Bill was doing quite well. He had slipped naturally into the ways of magpies, but did not associate with the Hills of Happiness crowd.

There was plenty of food around the hut and he lived there. During the day he prospected around the scrub and other bushland places and at night slept in the tree which contained the low branch, but nearer the top.

It was late winter when Bob came back to the hut. He arrived one night while Bill was fast asleep in his tree. The swagman had forgotten the bird during his wanderings, but as he lay in his bunk that night he wondered idly what had become of Bill. He fell asleep, still wondering. Bob was out of bed at the first flush of dawn and was just setting a light to his fire when, out of the gum tree came a melodious call that made him pause. The beautifully modulated notes rose and fell on the still morning air and the old swagman, who, in his time, had been serenaded a thousand times by magpies at dawn, listened in deep appreciation. It was music of which he could never tire.

"By jove," he said to himself, "I wonder could that be old Bill out there?"

He went to the door and threw it open. The magpie was still greeting the dawn with joyous warble.

"Hey, you, up in that tree!" roared Bob. "Is that you, Bill?"

The song stopped suddenly. There was a rustle of wings and a black-and-white hurricane swept to the ground and landed at the swagman's feet. It was certainly Bill! The bird rushed straight into the hut and hopped on to the table.

"Hey, dash me buttons, what's all the hurry about, Bill?" shouted Bob. Bill squawked in obvious delight as the old man hastily foraged around for something to give him. All he had was some corned meat, but Bill ate it rapidly.

"Well, Bill, you certainly look all right," he told his feathered friend. "Guess that Roddy feller has been mollycoddling you after all!"

Bill did not stay in the hut long. Presently he flew outside and perched on the low branch. Then he dropped to the ground and began to look for some additions to his breakfast. Corned meat was all right, but he preferred a tasty grasshopper or something like that.

Roddy was delighted to find old Bob back. Actually the swagman had been back for several days before the boy found out and in that time Bill had become part and parcel of the place. Roddy indignantly denied having mollycoddled the bird and told Bob what had happened.

"I guess we will have to put up with it," said Bob. "But Bill is too fine a bird to be hanging around a hut like a tramp cadging his tucker."

"How are you going to get rid of him then?" asked Roddy.

"I don't want to get rid of him. I like him around, but I'd prefer him in the trees always. I like people—and birds—to be independent," grunted the old man.

But Bob did not have to worry over Bill. That bird was no fool and neither was he dependent upon any human being for food or company. His was an affectionate nature, that was all. In addition to that, there was a far greater force than the old swagman could ever conjure up working and shaping the destiny of the black-and-white Bill.

One fine morning in mid-August, Bob was sitting outside mending his boots. Bill was hopping around the strip of grass not far from the hut door.

Then, from the very top of the gum tree over to the left, there came a magic burst of sweet magpie melody. The old swagman peered skywards and could just make out the shape of the singer.

"Friend of yours, Bill?" he asked, glancing at the bird on the grass.

Bill was standing stock-still, his beak pointing upwards. He was too absorbed in the song of the sweet charmer aloft to heed the old man. His feathers were gently quivering and he was making little chuckling noises.

"Aha, me lad!" grinned Bob. "Is that how it is, eh?"

Bill opened his wings and then closed them again. He seemed a little undecided what to do.

"Hey, what's wrong with you, you sissy!" said Bob. "Go and say good morning to the lady! Don't you know that no gentleman keeps a lady waiting?"

There came another burst of melody from the tree. Clearly, the other bird, a handsome black-and-white female, was making love to Bill, and that bashful bird couldn't make up his mind what to do.

"I'll make it up for you!" grunted Bob and towed a boot at Bill. The boot landed under his beak. Bill gave a startled squawk and hopped into the air.

"On your way, magpie," ordered Bob and made a rush at him. Bill sprang into the air and made a beeline for the top of the tree. Bob saw him come to rest at the side of the female songster, who looked at him closely and then rubbed her beak on his back. Bill returned the compliment.

"Why don't you kiss her?" howled old Bob.

Without deigning to reply to that, the female spread her wings and flew away, heading straight for the Hills of Happiness. After her, like a pied arrow, went Bill.

"And don't go chucking the young 'uns out of the nest and breaking their legs," the old swagman shouted after their retreating figures.

Then, with a loud and hearty laugh, he picked up the boot and resumed his mending.

Chapter XI
LENNIE THE LYREBIRD

ONE day- as Roddy was walking along a secluded bush track some distance from the bark hut, a big bird suddenly broke from the dense scrub and ran along the track before him. It was about the size a pheasant and had a long tail that drooped behind it. Roddy came to a halt and watched the bird run for some yards before it again darted back into the protecting scrub.

It took the boy some moments to realise that he had seen Menura, the lyre-bird—shyest of all the bush birds, sweet singer and mimic supreme.

Sometimes Roddy had heard Menura, or "Lennie" as he called the bird; or at least he thought he had. But he had always imagined that the graceful creature was deep in the bush. Recollecting that Lennie, as well as being a mimic, was something of a ventriloquist, the boy determined to search out its playground and watch it unobserved. He realised that this would be a very difficult task.

That evening, when he slipped over to the hut for a yarn with old Bob, he mentioned that he had seen the lyre-bird.

"Aye," nodded the swagman. "And I''ve been hearing

him. Why, the devil pulled my poor old leg properly the other night."

"A lyre-bird pulled your leg?" exclaimed the boy, thinking for a moment that Bob meant exactly what he said.

"Yes. It was about nine o'clock. I'd finished reading a magazine and was going to bed. Not long after I'd blown out the candle, I heard somebody chopping away at the big white gum behind the hut. 'Bless me,' I thought, 'who's gone mad now, chopping down trees in the middle of the night?'

"Anyway," continued Bob, "I crawled out of the bunk and sneaked round the hut to see who the lunatic was. It was bright moonlight, but I couldn't see a soul about. Thought it must have been a ghost or something, but then I heard the madman chopping wood up the hill. I took a stroll in that direction. Not a sign. Then I woke up to myself. It was that there lyre-bird, dash him!"

"He did pull your leg all right," laughed Roddy.

"Hold on," protested the swagman. "I'm not finished yet. Early this morning, about dawn it was, when an old stockwhip bird was lashing around good-oh, blow me if I didn't hear a train puffing uphill. It must be five miles to the railway, as you know, but there she was, a clear as anything, right alongside my bunk. Reckon old Lennie as you call him, must've been just through the bark wall. Then the train let out a whistle. I hopped out of bed to catch a glimpse at Lennie, but he wasn't there."

Next morning, while Roddy was bringing in the cows, he heard a beautifully clear whistle, the call of the rifle bird. He knew, however, that there were no rifle birds near. They were hidden far away in their own particular haunts. Next he heard the lovely song of Hook-beak, the butcher-bird, followed closely by the "clank-clank" of a currawong; and he realised that Lennie the lyre-bird was up to his tricks.

Roddy felt sure now that with patience and perseverance, he stood a chance of seeing Lennie in his playground. Evidently the dry weather had driven the birds down nearer the swamps and creeks.

After he had finished his share of the milking and had taken the cows back to their pasture, he prowled around in the bush, seeking the most likely place in which to find the lyre-bird. The search proved a long one, and he was feeling inclined to give it up until some other day, when he came across a tract of ground that had been cleared of fern, grass and twigs. In the centre was a mound of earth. There was no sign of any birds. Perhaps they had heard him coming and had made themselves scarce. He felt sure that he had found Lennie's playground, so he decided to creep out very early next morning and make his way to this spot unobserved.

Long before Ping the stockwhip bird had started to crack his whip, or Bill the magpie was carolling to the misty river, the boy was stealing with the utmost caution through the hush to the place where he hoped and trusted he would see Lennie dancing. Old Bob had told him that male lyre-birds danced on earth mounds before the admiring eyes of the hens.

When he had found the clearing again. he did not go near it but, finding a suitable tree, climbed to a low branch and hid behind the trunk, around which he could spy upon the birds—if they came. After a time he heard a sweet whistle, like that of Browneyes the thrush, and presently observed a bird, just like the creature he had seen on the bush track, run into the clearing from the bushes opposite. It made straight for the mound of earth and hopped lightly on to it. After him came three smaller birds, all hens.

As Roddy peeped around the concealing tree trunk, he saw Lennie spread his wonderful lyre-shaped tail and heard him whistle clear, sweet notes. His tail was twice his own bodily length and he stood with it high in the air, his head low. Then he strutted about, singing and whistling, imitating other bush birds while the hens watched him in admiration. Sometimes one of them would give an imitation, a particularly fine effort being a clear rendition of Jack Kookaburra's laugh, followed by the effective screech of Midnight, the black cockatoo.

By way of variation, Lennie launched into the harsh, buzzing scream of a circular saw cutting through a log. He followed this up by howling like a dingo and then, going from the ridiculous to the sublime, uttered the sweet call of a thrush at early morning.

There came an intermission to the performance when a hen bird marched into the clearing followed by a solitary chick. Roddy recalled that, according to old Bob, lyrebirds invariably laid only one egg at a time.

Lennie and his mates were a slaty-brown color, but only Lennie had the long, distinctive lyre-like tail feathers. The hens resembled ordinary fowls both in appearance and size, except that they possessed the sleek beauty of bush creatures — beauty never attained by domestic birds.

Having discovered the playground of the lyre-birds, Roddy's next move was to find their nest. He searched a great portion of the bushland without success and might have gone on indefinitely had not old Bob told him he was wasting his time.

"You won't find any lyre-bird's nests for months yet," said the wise old swagman. "They don't breed like other birds do, in the warm spring weather. Not them. They wait till the middle of winter."

"What on earth for?" exclaimed the boy.

"Not being a lyre-bird myself, I can't tell you," the old man chuckled. "However, I guess they have their reasons. It's my belief they do it so that by the time the youngsters are big enough to fend for themselves, danger from snakes and goannas will be past. Snakes sleep through the winter, you know. Lyre-birds' eggs take up to six weeks to hatch out and sometimes the young 'uns are in the nest for a couple of months."

"What are their nests like, Bob? I've never seen one," said Roddy.

"They build 'em of sticks and twigs, bark, dead leaves and so on. Sometimes they put 'em on the ground, or shove 'em in the fork of a tree. I saw one stuck in the hollow of a fern tree," replied the old chap.

One day, many weeks after this conversation, the boy was searching along the creek and the adjacent bush for a straying calf. It seemed a hopeless task because he did not know where the young animal had gone. At long last, in a gully, away from the open lands, he heard a faint mooing, as of a calf in pain.

Plunging into the thickets, the boy followed the sound, getting deeper and deeper into the gully but seeing no sign of the missing animal. Then he heard the faint mooing almost at his elbow and turned to look into a dense bit of scrub.

Out of the scrub ran a lyre-bird, right under his feet. It darted along the track and vanished. So, thought the lad, it was a lyre-bird giving imitations, and not his lost calf! It was, however, a clue, because surely a calf-call was a strange noise for a lyre-bird? The calf must have passed along this way for the bush mimic to hear it.

And so it proved. Roddy found the missing animal half-a-mile away from the spot where he had seen the lyre-bird.

Chapter XII
HOOK-BEAK, THE BUTCHER

IT was old Bob's fixed opinion that Hook-beak, butcher-bird, was nothing but a murderer.

"You take all the other killer-birds," he said Roddy. "They kill only when they are hungry, but butcher-birds kill at any time. They bowl over young birds, mice, lizards, beetles, grubs and so on, and instead of eating them, stick their bodies on thorns of high trees. They have larders just like butchers' shops."

"That shows their wisdom," Roddy protested. "They always have food on hand when times are hard."

"What about butcher-birds pulling the heads off tame canaries in cages?" retorted the swagman. "They know they can't take the bodies away, so they just kill the canaries for spite."

Roddy did not believe this, but he could not very well argue against Bob, because Hook-beak often hung around the farm trying to get at the canaries there. These canaries belonged to Roddy's father. Roddy did not believe in caging birds of any kind.

Hook-beak was a handsome bird, silver-grey in color, with a black cap and throat. He was a sweet singer, his notes ringing out in the early morning with singularly flute-like beauty. His nest was a large bowl-shaped structure of sticks and twigs lined with dry grass and other soft material. Roddy had seen several in various trees, and in Hook-beak's own there were three light greyish-green eggs with brown markings.

In spite of his murderous ways, old Bob's sanctuary would have been a dull place without Hook-beak.

Usually he and his mate kept together. Though a relative of Bill the magpie, the butchers did not live in colonies or attack passers-by in the nesting season after Bill's delightful little habit. As against that, Bill did not keep a larder of dead creatures.

Being so high from the ground, Hook-beak's own larder was fairly safe from thieves, such as wild or tame cats; not that these marauders would not have tried to secure the delicacies if they got the chance. They feared Hook-beak's claws and wicked bill too much to attempt anything.

There were, however, other enemies against which their weapons were not of much avail, and among these were the goannas. These rather slow-moving reptiles often climbed to great heights and if the top of any particular tree was broken off, they would go up and sun themselves on a levelled surface. Hook-beak and his mate had often fought off small goannas.

But one clear summer's morning, a large goanna—a big, ugly-looking brute—having smelled out the fresh meat spiked on the twigs aloft, decided to scale the tree to investigate.

As soon as Hook-beak saw his enemy, he flew at him, using beak and claws in an effort to divert the reptile's attention. They had little effect, however, because the goanna continued slowly up the trunk in a spiral movement. Hook-beak gave the loud warning call that summoned his mate to his assistance. She attacked with even greater fury, as mother birds will, and for a time it seemed that the intruder would be turned back. He clung to the tree trunk motionless for a long time, enduring the punishment, but waiting. The two birds flew and screamed around him and occasionally he snapped at them. But he did not retreat.

He moved at last, but farther up the tree. All the wild attacks and screams of the butcher-birds were in vain. Up and up he climbed and, reaching the larder, gobbled up the meat supply right in front of the butcher-birds' angry eyes. Filled with an insane rage, Hook-beak and his mate tore at his thick hide with savage beaks and claws, inflicting slight damage which did not seem to perturb the goanna at all. Nearing the ground he dropped from the trunk and lumbered clumsily away into the bush, while Hook-beak and his mate set off to replenish the plundered larder, flying in opposite directions.

In his roving, Hook-beak arrived at Roddy's farm and was immediately attracted by the canaries singing in the cage, which was hung in a shady corner.

Now it was a coincidence that a friend of Roddy's father was staying at the farm. He was an ornithologist, or bird-expert attached to a city museum, and he was in those parts for the purpose of collecting specimens of wild bird life. Roddy did not like him because of this, though the man had tried to explain to the boy the educational value of having samples of all birds in the museum. Roddy decided that the man would get no assistance from him.

The youngster was very glad that old Bob was away on the track, for if he found the stranger killing birds in his "sanctuary" there might be trouble.

Roddy was at school when Hook-beak came around the canary cage this day. The ornithologist, however, was there, and coming out of the house unexpectedly, he saw Hook-beak hanging to the wire of the canary cage. The bird flew off when he saw the man, but the ornithologist knew he would be back. And he intended to have a fitting welcome prepared.

He made a trap. It was a simple thing of wire with a trapdoor and he placed it on top of the canary cage. Then he hid from view. Back came the butcher-bird and he fell for the trap straight away. Seeing in it a way into the canary cage, he jumped in without a second thought, the lid closing with a snap. When he found himself confined behind wires, he went mad, dashing himself against the sides and screaming loudly until his mate came frantically along to see what the trouble was.

The ornithologist decided that a pair of butcher-birds would be better than a single specimen, so he removed Hook-beak and his trap and set another in its place. But Mrs. Hook-beak was too wily and refused to enter the trap. Possibly her mate had warned her to keep away. The trapper gave it up and as he was going off into the distant bush camping for a few days, left the trap, and Hook-beak, at the farm to pick up on his return. Then, he said, he would kill the butcher-bird and prepare its body for the museum along with his other specimens—if he caught any.

When Roddy came home from school and was told what had happened, he was most indignant.

"But this man can't take Hook-beak away," he protested. "The bird belongs to old Bob's sanctuary."

"Well, he's got him in the cage safely enough, and I'm glad," said Roddy's mother. "Now we won't be afraid to leave the canaries outside all day."

"But Hook-beak isn't the only butcher-bird in the bush!" exclaimed the boy. "What is the use of his taking one? He'd have to take them all to make the canaries safe. Anyway, I hope old Hook-beak escapes."

"There will be trouble on this farm if you let that bird out, Roddy," warned his father sternly.

"Of course I wouldn't let Hook-beak out, but he might get out of his own accord," said the boy, and went out to the cage to give the bird some pieces of raw meat.

Early next morning when Roddy again went to the cage, Hook-beak wasn't there. Roddy heard him carolling happily in his flute-like voice away in the bush near his larder which he was busily replenishing. Perhaps he was also telling his mate all about the trap he had fallen into.

At breakfast, the lad's mother asked him, "Roddy, what did you do to the butcher-bird's cage? He got out, as I suppose you know."

"Did he really?" asked the boy innocently. "Then that must have been him I heard whistling so merrily this morning."

"Do you know how he got out?" she asked sternly.

"I can guess. What was the use of the man tying the case door with string? Hook-beak would think it was good material to repair his nest and would pull it off. Then the door would open."

And that is what had happened, except that on the previous night when Roddy had taken Hook-beak out his raw meat, he had taken the wire off the cage door and substituted string. He hated to see wild birds in cages.

Chapter XIII
BLUE EYES, THE BOWER BIRD

ON the river flats bordering the swamps, far away from the farmhouse, stood a Moreton Bay fig tree, a solitary giant with great, twisted roots rising like bastions to become part of its mighty trunk. Nobody remembered how long the tree, the sole representative of its kind, had been there, or how it had got there in the first place. Its boughs reached out many yards on every side, giving shade to stock that grazed in the vicinity. In its great heart, birds found shelter from the heat of summer and from rain and gales in winter.

To Roddy, the tree had a peculiar fascination, and he often spent long hours among its branches. Sometimes he would take his lunch there and eat it in the quite shade.

A corner post of a fence stood about twenty feet from the old tree trunk and in the smaller paddock so formed, the ground was so rocky and hard that stock never ran on it. But near this corner post was long, tussock grass, alternating with level clearings. It was there, one summer's day, that Roddy first saw the bower-birds.

The boy had been on a long tramp seeking the nest of Boomer the bittern in the swamps, but hadn't found it. He had his lunch with him, and climbed on to a low bough in the fig tree to eat. His eye was attracted by a movement among the tussocks and he saw a bird with beautiful satin-like plumage run out of the grass, dart about, then turn and run back to shelter. His eyes almost popped out of his head. A bower-bird! He had not the least idea that these birds were anywhere in the vicinity.

As Roddy watched, he saw another bird, with the same shining blue plumage as the first, dance out into the open, pirouette about and then run back as the first had done. Even from his vantage point, he could see that the bird's eyes were violet-blue, so he named it at once, in his queer little way, "Blue-eyes the bower bird."

Examining the place as closely as he could, the boy discovered that what looked like mere clumps of grass were really tunnels, about a foot high, the tops being looped together and held by fibres woven through them to make the bowers from which the birds derived their names. Now and again Roddy noticed some birds of duller plumage moving about in the bowers, and knew, from what old Bob had told him, that these were the hens before which the males had been dancing to show off their charms.

Eventually Roddy became so excited that he lost his balance on the low branch and crashed to earth. The show was over, the bower birds vanishing completely. Picking himself up and rubbing his legs ruefully, the boy walked carefully to the playground to examine it. It was much larger than he expected. In the sheltered corner near the post, the birds had built an elaborate bower. The floor was thickly covered with interlaced sticks and where tall grass grew, the tops were laced together about nine inches from the ground. From the main runs others branched, the whole forming a miniature labyrinth.

The birds had collected bright objects from the bush—feathers, flowers, pretty stones, shells, tiny bones polished by wind and rain, pieces of tin, old rifle cartridges, bits of glass and such other odds and ends that they could find. Roddy could not help but notice that the favorite color of the birds was blue. A piece of blue paper from an old jam tin hung from twigs and a bit of blue glass lay on the ground at the corner where two runs met. The earth was so worn at the spot that it appeared as if the birds spent a lot of time there admiring this glass.

Though he waited a long time in the hope that the birds would return, there was no sign of them when the setting sun warned him that it was time he went home to get the cows for the evening milking.

One early morning he took his sister Susan down to watch the birds at play. They saw handsome, satin-plumaged Blue-eyes dash out of a run carrying a blue flower in his beak, turn round and run back in. Out he dashed again, but this time he darted around the bower to find another opening.

Having seen the birds' playground, the boy could not, of course, rest contented until he had found their nest. By patient exploration, he discovered one, far away from the bower. It was in a low bush in a secluded spot. Constructed of sticks and roughly cup-shaped, it held two cream-colored eggs blotched and spotted with brown and grey.

That night at the evening meal, Roddy told his father about the nest.

"I hope you pulled the thing to pieces," said his father.

"Good gracious, no!" exclaimed the horrified boy. "Why should I do that?"

His father laughed good-humoredly and winked at his mother.

"Bower birds are among the worst fruit thieves in the world," he said. "They'd strip a tree in a night if they were allowed."

"Bower birds will?" exclaimed the boy.

"No doubt about that, my lad."

"But surely you wouldn't go and shoot a bower bird?" cried the frantic boy. "Why, they are so—so..." He paused, unable to find words adequately to express his admiration of such ingenious creatures.

"All right then, Rod," said his father kindly. "I was only joking. We won't kill your bower birds. We'll reserve a special peach tree for them, eh?"

"If you saw Blue-eyes, you'd just love him," said the boy.

"Oh, sure, sure," laughed his father. "Let it go at that."

"But he's so—so beautiful," Roddy raved. He was so earnest that he made even Susan laugh.

Chapter XIV
BOOMER THE BITTERN

AT NIGHT the swamps were lonely, stretching away in the darkness, eerie and mysterious. Roddy, of course, never went there alone after dark, for there were stories of strange creatures that once lived in the murky waters. Perhaps they were still there. From old Bob he had heard stories which the old swagman had told him were just fairy yarns, of the bunyip, and the Gumperthing which pounced from behind bulrushes and laid turtle's eggs in the platypus's nest. Also stories of queer birds and queerer beasts not nice to meet in the dark when you were on your own.

And as if to prove that there were such things, the voice of Boomer the bittern rang out in the evenings and continued until midnight, the witching hour, when even the frogs ceased creaking. Coucal, the swamp pheasant, also had a queer call—something like a bull-frog with a secret sorrow.

Coucal, if he felt that way, had no cause to laugh at any other bird, because he was a bit queer himself. First of all he was a cuckoo, but unlike others of that species, he actually built a nest, choosing a grass tussock, his head sticking out one end and his tail the other. And though he sometimes ate grasshoppers and other insects like the cuckoos, he also favored lizards, mice and frogs. If they were too large to swallow in one gulp he held them in his claws and tore them to bits with his beak. And as for his voice, well, it was like water being poured out of a bottle.

Other birds were swamp-denizens, such as the cormorants, the pelicans and the straw-necked ibis. Roddy always imagined the ibis as having stepped from a picture of old Egypt. Somehow the bird had a foreign look; but his habits were not foreign. He was one of the best grasshopper killers in the country.

There was a flat-bottomed boat tied up on the farm side of the swamp, but it could only be used when the swamps were filled with water. They filled in much the same way as a billabong, by overflow from the river. The boat was used chiefly to rescue cattle or sheep that had wandered away among the rushes and reeds and become bogged. Roddy had been all over the swamps with his father in the boat by day. He had seen Bluey the crane, a beautiful long-legged heron with white breast-feathers and a long black bill. When disturbed, Bluey rose slowly on huge wings that seemed scarcely able to bear his weight because they flapped so slowly; yet he soon disappeared—to alight upon a sheltered portion of the swamps where he could fish undisturbed by human intruders.

There was, too, Nankeen, the night heron. Roddy had had only a glimpse of him. It was at dusk one summer afternoon.

At night, sometimes, and more especially when the moon was full, Roddy would walk down to the edge of the swamp and listen to the noises from its mysterious expanse—croaking of frogs, the screeching calls of Long-neck the grebe, shriller sounds from herons or cranes, but, over it all, the booming of the bitterns. The boom seemed to travel along the water from a great distance. Almost as eerie were the queer voices of hunting frogmouths and nightjars.

There had been a fresh in the river and the overflow had filled the swamps. One day old Bob mentioned the fact to Roddy.

"You are always moaning about not having seen Boomer the bittern, my lad," said the swagman. "How would you like to look him up to-night?"

The boy's eyes gleamed.

"Truly? Would you take me?" he asked excitedly.

"Yes, if there's no objections at home," said Bob.

"There won't be when they know you will be with me," said Roddy.

"All right then. Be down at the boat when the moon rises. It's no good going in the dark. We couldn't see anything. The swamp people like the moonlight and come out to enjoy it."

As they pushed off in the old boat, the light was dim, but it would soon be brighter because it was the night of the full moon. Roddy sat in the stern while old Bob rowed slowly. The lad was thrilled. The swamps around him seemed to ooze the mystery of nameless things. Though there were many living creatures around, the only ones that advertised their presence were the frogs, and they did so lustily.

A deep, booming sound echoed across the water.

"That's old Boomer," Bob said. "We ought to get a

peep at him soon. Pretty hard to see when you do locate him. The way birds hide is marvellous. Right around us are hundreds of them, but you wouldn't guess it if you didn't know. It just looks like an empty swamp, except, of course, for those noisy frogs."

A nightjar went past above them on wings that made not the slightest sound.

"I guess old frogmouth will get a feed to-night," observed Bob.

"Owls and nightjars and frogmouths are cruel things," said the boy.

"If killing insects, mice, rats and frogs is cruel, they certainly are," said Bob.

"But they kill young birds too," said Roddy.

"Not many, sonny boy."

As they rowed along talking in subdued voices, the moon rose in all her majestic splendor. Far away towards the hills came the "wee-lo" of the stone-curlew, ghostly and faint, mingling with the cries of other night creatures heralding the moon. Then Roddy's heart missed a beat as a call came, very close, which seemed to make the water tremble.

"That's old Boomer," whispered Bob, ceasing to row. "He's not far from here. Listen!"

As they sat very still, the only sounds were the ripple of the water at the bows and the far-away call of the curlew. Once again rang out the booming sound and old Bob whispered: "He hasn't heard us and he's very close. Don't move. We're drifting nearer."

Sooner than he anticipated, Roddy heard the old man whisper the words that made him quiver with excitement:

"There he is, Roddy—look! See that old stick with a thin top and a thick middle, like a broken branch?"

"Yes," the boy whispered back. "Is Boomer behind it?"

"No. That's Boomer in person. He stands like that to look like a small dead tree."

"Is that him?" demanded the boy. His tone had so much disgust in it that old Bob laughed aloud. It broke the silence. In an instant the small dead tree unbent and a big bird dashed away, splashing in the shallow water. Boomer had taken flight.

"Now do you believe me?" demanded the swagman. Roddy said he did, and was loud in his thanks to the old man for having caused him to realise a pet ambition. He had, at last, seen Boomer.

When they got back to the landing, the moon rode high and clear over the swamps and bushland, shedding its soft, white radiance impartially. On the running river it glittered where rocky bars churned the water into white foam.

"Isn't everything so wonderful, Bob?" asked the boy as he took the old man's hand.

"It surely is," the old wanderer replied. "And how few people ever see it. They would not sit in their stuffy old picture theatres seeing it all at second hand on the movie screen if they knew it was here for nothing. Yes, lad, it certainly is grand—the bush, the hills, the river, the open lands and even the swamps. God made them all, Roddy."

"Yes, Bob, just as He made all the children in your own sanctuary."

At the place where the tracks branched, one leading to the farm and the other to the old bush hut, the boy said,

"Good night, Bob. Thank you very much for taking me to see old Boomer."

"Don't thank me, lad," replied the old swagman. "Thank your lucky stars that we were able to get so close to him."

"Good night, son," he added. "I'm off on the track to-morrow. But I'll be back in the spring. So-long and the best of luck."

"And oceans of good luck to you, Bob," replied Roddy affectionately.

THE END.

www.ingramcontent.com/pod-product-compliance
Lightning Source LLC
Chambersburg PA
CBHW072147020426
42334CB00018B/1912